THE Persians

BY ÆSCHYLUS

PRENTICE-HALL GREEK DRAMA SERIES

Series Editors

ERIC A. HAVELOCK, *Sterling Professor of Classics, Yale University*
MAYNARD MACK, *Sterling Professor of English, Yale University*

AESCHYLUS	Translated with commentary by
Agamemnon	Hugh Lloyd-Jones
The Eumenides	Hugh Lloyd-Jones
The Libation Bearers	Hugh Lloyd-Jones
The Persians	Anthony J. Podlecki
Prometheus Bound	Eric A. Havelock
The Seven Against Thebes	Christopher M. Dawson

SOPHOCLES	
Ajax	Adam M. Parry
Antigone	Anne Amory
Electra	William Sale
Oedipus at Colonus	Joseph A. Russo
Oedipus the King	Thomas Gould
Philoctetes	William Arrowsmith
The Women of Trachis	Peter W. Rose

EURIPIDES	
Alcestis	Charles Rowan Beye
The Bacchae	Geoffrey S. Kirk
Electra	Wesley Smith
Heracles	Christian Wolff
Hippolytus	Gilbert & Sally Lawall
Ion	Anne Pippin Burnett
Iphigenia in Aulis	Kenneth Cavander
Medea	Bernard M. W. Knox
The Suppliants	A. Thomas Cole

The remaining nine plays are in preparation.

THe Persians

BY æSCHYLUS

A Translation with Commentary by

ANTHONY J. PODLECKI

Professor of Classics
Pennsylvania State University

with a series introduction by Eric A. Havelock

PRENTICE-HALL, INC., ENGLEWOOD CLIFFS, N.J.

PRENTICE-HALL INTERNATIONAL, INC. *London*
PRENTICE-HALL OF AUSTRALIA, PTY. LTD. *Sydney*
PRENTICE-HALL OF CANADA, LTD. *Toronto*
PRENTICE-HALL OF INDIA PRIVATE LIMITED *New Delhi*
PRENTICE-HALL OF JAPAN, INC. *Tokyo*

G. ET G.
AFFINIBUS ATQUE AMICIS

CONTENTS

FOREWORD TO THE SERIES

The Prentice-Hall Greek Drama Series will contain when completed the surviving tragedies of the Athenian stage. It offers each play in a separate inexpensive volume, so that readers may make their own personal selection rather than have the choice made for them, as is commonly the result when translations are issued in collective groups. It also offers each play in a context of exacting scholarship which seeks to make available to Greekless readers what the original Greek audiences responded to as they watched and listened to a performance. Under the English dress, in short, as far as humanly possible the Greek identity has been accentuated rather than obscured. Supported here by extensive introductions, notes, and appendices (in each case the work of an authority who has given painstaking attention to the full meanings of the text) and printed in a manner to exhibit their great varieties of formal structure, they step forth, untrammeled by preconceptions and conventional categorizations, as the highly individual creations they were when first performed.

The notes printed at the foot of each page to accompany the appropriate lines are in the first instance conceived as a corrective to shortcomings that no translation can avoid and should therefore be considered as in some sense an extension of the text. They testify to the fact that all translations in varying degree must indulge an element of deception, and they serve as a running attempt to explain its character and define its extent. In addition to this, they undertake to instruct the reader about conventions of idiom and imagery, of legend and allusion, which are native to the Greek situation and indispensable to a proper understanding of it. They aim also to get to the heart of the play as a work of art, exposing and explicating its often complex design in the hope that the reader thus aided will experience for himself its overwhelming dramatic effect.

M. M.

THE ATHENIAN DRAMATISTS

(Dates attested or probable are italicized)

AESCHYLUS	SOPHOCLES	EURIPIDES
525–456	*497/6–405/4*	*485/4–406/5*
Total production: c.90	Total production: c.125	Total production: c.92
Surviving plays: 7	Surviving plays: 7*	Surviving plays: 17*
First success *485*	First success *469*	First success *441*

AESCHYLUS

The Persians 472
The Seven Against Thebes 467
The Suppliants 463?

Oresteia 458
(*Agamemnon, The Libation Bearers, The Eumenides*)
Prometheus Bound (date unknown probably late)

SOPHOCLES

Ajax 460–45?
(date unknown— probably the earliest)

Antigone 442–41

The Women of Trachis (date unknown)

Oedipus the King 429–25?

Electra 420–10

Philoctetes 409

Oedipus at Colonus c. 406–5 (produced posthumously)

EURIPIDES

Alcestis 438
Medea 431
The Children of Heracles c. 430–20
Hippolytus 428
Hecuba c. 425
The Suppliants c. 420
Heracles c. 420–16?
Andromache c. 419
Electra c. 415–13
The Trojan Women 415
Helen 412
Iphigeneia in Tauris c. 412
The Phoenician Women 410–9

Orestes 408
Ion c. 408?
The Bacchae c. 406 (produced posthumously)
Iphigeneia at Aulis 406 (produced posthumously)

* disregarding *The Ichneutae* of Sophocles and *The Cyclops* and *Rhesus* of Euripides which are not tragedies.

INTRODUCTION TO THE SERIES

1. GREEK TRAGEDY TODAY

The table of the three tragedians and their productions facing this page reveals a situation which, judged by our experience of European drama since the Greeks, is, to say the least, unusual. The total of thirty-one plays was composed within a span of about sixty-five years, between 472 and 406 B.C., and that ends the story. It is as though the history of the English drama were confined to the Elizabethans and the Jacobeans and then closed. These thirty-one are survivors—a mere handful—of an originally enormous total. The three playwrights between them are credited with over three hundred titles, and the plays of their competitors, which except for isolated fragments and notices have now vanished from the record, are uncountable.

These facts shed light upon a familiar paradox: Classic Greek drama is at once parochial and universal, narrowly concentrated upon recurrent motifs, characters, and situations, yet always able to evoke a response at a level which is fundamental and general. Most of these hundreds of plays were composed in the years between the defeat of the Persians by the Greeks at Salamis in 480 B.C. and the defeat of Athens by Sparta in 404 B.C.; they were produced for audiences in Athens and in Attica, that small canton district which contains the city and is itself circumscribed by the sea and the mountains. The limits of history and geography surrounding them are therefore narrow and intense. Greek tragedy is Attic and Athenian not accidentally but essentially, and this fact cannot but have had strong influence in the dramatic choices made by the playwrights as they selected situation, theme, and characters. The vast bulk of the lost productions, had it been preserved, would, one suspects, retain interest today mainly for specialists and antiquarians. There is indeed a good deal of antiquarianism in the plays we do have. But they are products of their authors' maturity, none composed at an age earlier than forty-five. Their preservation, if we except a few plays of Euripides, reflects some value judgments passed in antiquity; they were on the whole better able to withstand changes of taste and fashion and shifts in the character and nationality of audiences and critics.

The present age has come to recognize a new-found affinity with them. During the last century and the early part of the present one, when study of the classics was still dominant in education, Greek drama was read and esteemed as an exercise in the grand style, a mirror of the eternal verities and familiar moral imperatives. Even Euripides, the least tractable of the three from the moral standpoint, was credited with a desire to set the world right. By and large, the watchword the Victorians heard in the plays was not danger but decorum. Today, a generation which has known frustration and disillusionment—desperately demanding some private identity within a society which seems imprisoned and perhaps doomed by its own prior commitments—can view these plays with clearer eyes for what they are: portrayals of the human dilemma which forswear the luxury of moral confidence and assured solutions. Here are sufferings disproportionate to the original error, characters caught and trapped in situations which are too much for them and for which they are only partly responsible. Here are pity and terror treated as facts of life with which one must come to terms. Here finally is defiance combined with a fatalism which accepts the tragic scene even at the moment of its repudiation. The watchword we listen to today is not decorum but danger. For the children of men who now inherit the earth it is therefore possible to respond to the classic tragedy of the Greeks with a directness denied to the more secure temper of their forebears.

Translators of Greek drama face a difficult choice between editing the Greek into language which will appeal to the modern sensibility, or offering a version which attempts as close an approximation as possible to the form and content of the original. The present series has been conceived on the assumption that since form and content hang together, the one cannot be paraphrased without damaging the other. The damage usually is done by suppressing those features of the original which affront the modern sensibility, while exaggerating those that do not. Quite commonly the operatic form of the plays is in a modern version played down or even ignored, and the temptation is always strong so to interpret the plots as to center interest upon characters at the expense of situation. The versions offered in this series, while modest in their pretensions, have sought to maintain fidelity to that original convention of the Greek which divided the diction of a play between choric and lyric portions on the one hand and spoken dialogue on the other. The two together constituted the total dramatic statement, which was thus partly sung and partly recited, and they are here printed in different typefaces to bring out more clearly the way in which the play's structure is articulated. Passages in hexameters, anapests, and trochaic tetrameters were either sung or chanted, and accordingly are printed here as lyric. The notes also make some attempt to indicate the metrical arrangements practiced in the lyric portions and the emotional effects produced. To transfer these effects in translation from an inflected tongue quantitatively scanned is impossible, and the aids offered are therefore directed to the imagination of the reader rather than to his ear.

2. THE DRAMATISTS

The alienation of the artist is not a condition which the Greeks of the classical age would readily have understood. The three Greek tragedians were Attic born and men of their time, participating, as the record indicates, in the political and social life of their community. Their plays accordingly expose, examine, and question the values of Greek society, but they do not reformulate and they do not reject. This being said, one must add that differences of style and approach between them are marked. The grandiloquence of Aeschylus becomes an appropriate instrument for expressing the confident ethos of the Athenian democracy and a theology which would justify the ways of Zeus to men. In the more stringent style of Sophocles, the tragic hero and heroine endure an exposure which is often ironic but which penetrates to the core of their dilemma, while their essential dignity is preserved and even enhanced. Euripides, the "most tragic" of the three, comes nearest to stepping outside his society. His later plays in particular tend to place the traditional norms of heroic and aristocratic leadership in an equivocal light. But his plots, as they enlarge the roles of women, children, servants, and slaves, remain faithful also to the changing mores and manners which increasingly foreshadowed the individualism of the Hellenistic age.

AESCHYLUS was born c. 525–24 at Eleusis near Athens of an aristocratic family (*eupatrid*). At thirty-five he fought at Marathon, where his brother fell gloriously; he may have also fought at Salamis. He paid two visits to the court of Hieron in Sicily, who was the patron likewise of Pindar, Bacchylides, and Simonides. At the first visit he composed a play for the court celebrating Hieron's founding of the new city of Aetna (after 476); the second visit was terminated by his death at Gela in his seventieth year (456), where an epitaph on his monument celebrated his service at Marathon. An Athenian decree subsequently provided for the revival of any of his plays at public expense. Though he was preceded in the composition of tragic drama by the semi-legendary Thespis, Aeschylus is for practical purposes the "founder" of this unique art form, combining choric performance with a plot supported by dialogue between two, later three, actors. He was both composer and actor-manager, taking leads himself in some of his plays, probably the early ones. He is credited with developing the conventions of grandiloquent diction, rich costuming, formal dance figures, and some degree of spectacular effect. Although he died only about fifty years before *The Frogs* appeared, by Aristophanes' day his life was already a legend. Later stories about him (e.g., that he was an "initiate" who betrayed the secret of the Mysteries, or that he retired to Sicily in discomfiture for a variety of alleged reasons) are probably the inventions of an age more biographically inclined than his own.

SOPHOCLES was born c. 496 of an affluent family at Colonus near Athens. Known for his good looks, he was also an accomplished dancer and lyre player who, at age sixteen, was selected to lead the paean of victory after Salamis. He was taught by Lamprus, a famous master of the traditional music. He played roles in some of his own early productions, but later desisted, because of his weak voice. He took considerable part in public life. In 443–42 he was imperial treasurer; he was elected general twice —once in 440, the year in which Pericles suppressed the revolt of Samos, and again at a later date as colleague of Nicias; also, in 413, when he was over eighty years old, he was appointed one of the special commissioners (*probouloi*) to review the aftermath of the Sicilian disaster. He held a lay priesthood in the cult of a local deity of healing and allowed his own house to serve as a shrine of Asclepius pending the completion of a temple. He founded an Association (*thiasos*) of the Muses (something like a literary club). Polygnotus painted a portrait of him holding the lyre, which was hung in the picture gallery on the Acropolis. Tradition connects him with prominent men of letters, such as Ion of Chios, Herodotus (there are discernible points of contact between the History and the plays), and Archelaus the philosopher. In 406 he mourned the death of his younger contemporary Euripides in a public appearance with actors and chorus at the rehearsal (*proagon*) for the Great Dionysia. Some months later he died, at the age of ninety. He was remembered and celebrated as an example of the fortunate life, genial, accomplished, and serene.

EURIPIDES was born c. 485 at Phlya in Attica, probably of a good family. He made his home in Salamis, probably on an estate of his father, where it is said he composed in a cave by the sea. He held a lay priesthood in the cult of Zeus at his birthplace. Tradition, supported by hints in Old Comedy and the internal evidence of his own plays, connects him with the leading sophistic and philosophical circles of the day: Anaxagoras, Archelaus, Prodicus, Protagoras, and above all Socrates, said to be an admirer of his plays. In musical composition, he was assisted by a certain Cephisophon; this collaboration was probably a common practice. He served on an embassy to Syracuse (date unknown) and composed a public elegy in 413 for the Athenian soldiers fallen in Sicily. Prisoners in the quarries are said to have won release from their captors by reciting his choruses. He appears to have preferred a life of some seclusion, surrounded by his household. In 408-7 he left Athens for the north. He stayed initially at Magnesia in Thessaly, where he was received with honors, and then at the court of Archelaus of Macedon. There, in addition to a court play composed in the king's honor, he produced *The Bacchae*, his last extant work. He died there in 406. Buried in Macedonia he was memorialized by a cenotaph at Athens. Some of his plays were produced posthumously by one of his three sons. A good deal of the tradition surrounding his parentage, domestic life, personal character, and contemporary reputation in Athens is unfriendly to him; but it is also unreliable, depending as it probably does on the satirical treatment which he often received from the comic poets.

3. THE TIMES

In 525, when Aeschylus was born, the "tyranny" established at Athens under Pisistratus and his sons was still in power. When he was fifteen years old, the tyrants were expelled, and a series of constitutional changes began which were to result in the establishment of complete democracy.

Abroad, the Persian Empire, founded by Cyrus the Great, had already absorbed all of Asia Minor and extended its sway over the Ionian Greeks. The year of Aeschylus' birth had been marked by the Persian conquest of Egypt, followed by that of Babylon. When he was twenty-six, the Ionian Greeks revolted against their Persian masters, were defeated and partially enslaved (494), after which the Persian power sought to extend its conquests to the Greek mainland. This attempt, repulsed at Marathon (490), was finally defeated at Salamis, Plataea, and Mycale (480–79). The Greeks in turn, under the leadership of Athens, liberated the Ionians from Persian control and established the Confederacy of Delos to preserve the liberty thus gained.

By degrees, this alliance was transformed into the Athenian Empire, governed by an ascendant and confident democracy, under the leadership of many eminent men, none more so than Pericles, whose political power lasted from about 460 to his death in 429. The empire, though supported as a defense against Persia, became the natural target of disaffected allies, who found themselves becoming subjects, and of the jealousy of other Greek states, notably Sparta and Corinth. In 432 a Peloponnesian coalition under Spartan leadership opened hostilities with Athens, ostensibly to free Greece from her yoke. The war lasted, with an interval of armistice, till 404, when Athens, exhausted and over-extended by commitments, lost her last naval protection and was besieged and captured by the Peloponnesian forces.

Within the two years preceding this event, Euripides and Sophocles had both died. The works of the three dramatists were therefore composed during an expansive age in which democracy at home was matched by imperialism abroad. The repulse of the foreign invader was followed by the extension of Athenian commerce and influence throughout the eastern Mediterranean, and to some extent in the west also. This brought in the revenues and also encouraged the confidence in leadership which supported Pericles' ambitious policies and adorned the Acropolis with those public buildings, unmatched in purity of style, which still stand there.

But before the last plays were written, the strain of an exhausting and demoralizing war with fellow Greeks was beginning to tell, and in a moment of crisis even the democratic constitution had been called in question (411). For Aeschylus, his city's history had been an unbroken success story. In the lifetime of his two successors, she confronted an

increasing series of problems, military, political, and social, which proved
too much even for her energies to sustain.

4. GREEK THEATRICAL PERFORMANCE

The twelfth chapter of Aristotle's *Poetics* contains the following
statement:

> . . . The quantitative sections . . . into which a tragedy is divided
> are the following: *prologos, epeisodion, exodos,* and the choral part,
> itself subdivided into *parodos* and *stasima.* These occur in all
> tragedies; there may also be actors' songs and *kommoi.*
>
> The *prologos* is that whole section which precedes the en-
> trance of the chorus; the *epeisodion* is a whole section between
> complete choral odes; the *exodos* is that whole section of a tragedy
> which is not followed by a choral ode. In the choral part, the en-
> trance song (*parodos*) is the first complete statement of the chorus,
> a *stasimon* is a song of the chorus without anapests or trochees; a
> *kommos* is a dirge in which actors and chorus join. . . .*

Students in English literature and other fields are likely to have
been introduced to this famous passage. Yet scarcely any statement about
Greek drama has caused more misunderstanding. It is schematic when
it should be tentative, and definitive when it should be approximate. It
has encouraged the presumption, widely held, that Greek plays were
constructed according to a standard model from which, to be sure, the
dramatist might diverge on occasion, but which nevertheless was his
model. A prologue was followed by a choric entrance, for which anapests
were supposedly the normal vehicle, and this by dialogue divided into
episodes separated by full choruses, and concluded by an exit after the
last chorus. No doubt the anonymous author (Aristotle could scarcely
have been so dogmatic or so wrong) reflects those standards of mechani-
cal formalism current in the period of the drama's decline. The key
statement, "These occur in all tragedies," is false. The suggestion that
actors' songs and *kommoi* (duets, trios, and quartets) were additions to
the standard form is equally false. In Aeschylus alone, the reader will
discover that neither his *The Persians* nor his *The Suppliants* has either

---

* Translation by G. M. A. Grube, from *Aristotle on Poetry and Style.* New
York: Liberal Arts Press, 1958.

prologos or *exodos* (applying these terms as defined in the *Poetics*). If the *Prometheus Bound* has a *parodos*, it is technically a *kommos*, that is, a duet shared between Prometheus and the chorus. Two of the *stasima*, or choric odes, in *The Eumenides* are interrupted by nonchoric iambics. It would be interesting to know how the author of these remarks would apply his definition of *exodos* to *Agamemnon*. On his terms, the *exodos* extends from lines 1035 to 1673, but it includes one elaborate lyric duet sung by Cassandra and chorus, then the murder of Agamemnon, then an equally elaborate duet sung by Clytemnestra and chorus. The *parodos* of *The Seven Against Thebes* is not in anapests, nor is that of *The Eumenides*, and the *exodos* of *The Eumenides* is, in effect, an elaborate lyric trio shared between Athena and two different choruses.

No doubt the practice of Sophocles encouraged schematization, but even his practice often included in the *exodos* the climactic portions of the drama. *Oedipus the King* is an example. The practice of Euripides often reverts to the fluidity characteristic of Aeschylus. The fact seems to be that the whole conception of a tragedy as consisting of quantitative parts is erroneous, and the reader is best advised to approach each play as, in some sense, a new creation. Hence, though translators in this series may from time to time use the classic, or neoclassic, terms of the *Poetics*, they may equally be forced to apply modern terminology and speak of choric or lyric songs, of acts and scenes, of entrances, exits, and finales, according as the specific structure of any given play may require.

The conditions of production have never since been duplicated, and since they affect the way the plays were written, a word about them is in order. Performances took place in the open air. The audience sat on benches inserted into the slope of a recessed hillside. Chorus and actors shared not a stage but a circular dancing floor, on which the audience looked down. Thus, the Greek play remained a spectacle for the eye, as well as a verbal and musical delight to the ear, particularly as the figures executed in the dances produced patterns which an elevated angle of vision could appreciate. The audience was rarely asked to imagine the action as taking place in a closed room. Forecourts and courtyards and the street itself predominate as settings under the Mediterranean sky, and that sky itself, as the reader will discover, is never very far away from the characters' thought and speech.

At the back of the dancing floor stood a temporary wooden structure, the proscenium, with a central and two side doors and a flat roof. The doors were used for entrances and exits, the roof as a platform for appearances that called for an elevated position (those of gods, and sometimes human beings like the Watchman in the opening scene of *Aga-*

memnon). Behind the proscenium the actors could change their costumes, which were formalized to indicate sex, age, and social status. It is important to distinguish the *characters* who appear in a given play from the *actors* who played their parts. The former, while few by Shakespearean standards, considerably outnumbered the latter, who were rationed to two in some plays, three in most (four occasionally and doubtfully). The practical effect was that not more than two or three speaking parts could be carried on at any one time, so that at least some of the characters had to be played by different actors at different times, and the actors, relying on costume changes, had to be prepared to change their roles with rapidity. This ancient convention had an important result: The personality of the actor was severed from the role he played—this was also an effect of his mask—and reduced in importance (that is, until conventions changed in the Hellenistic age); and hence the burden of dramatic emphasis had to be carried entirely by the language, whoever happened to be speaking it. This is one reason why the verbal virtuosity of Greek tragedy has never been surpassed, even by Shakespeare.

The limitation of actors to two or three was undoubtedly related to a practical necessity. To examine (as one can do very easily in the typography employed in this series) the proportions of lyric to dialogue in a Greek play—that is, of sung to spoken parts, as these are assigned to individual actors (ignoring the chorus)—is to discover that the actors, and not just the chorus, had to have excellent singing voices enabling them to sustain solos, duets, trios and quartets. Even if they were assigned on a trial basis—the precise details of selection are disputable— the supply of suitable voices would be limited, and would require rationing among several plays competing simultaneously.

The standard phrase to describe authorship was "to teach a chorus," while "to grant a chorus" indicated the procedures of acceptance which put a play in production. Both seem to argue for the priority of the chorus in the classic Greek conception though the degree of priority is again a matter of dispute. The assembling and training of a group of singers and dancers (the total number is in dispute and may have varied) obviously took the most time, money, and skill. The expense was borne partly by the state and partly by private patrons, though the arrangements changed somewhat in the course of time. The playwright became his own producer, exercising a degree of control which is reflected in the tight unity of most Greek plays, exhibiting as they do something of the symmetry of Greek architecture.

The lyrics were accompanied by woodwinds, and the anapests, trochaic tetrameters, and dactyls were chanted, very possibly to the accompaniment of strings. The term chorus, however, indicates not singers but dancers, just as the terms strophe and antistrophe (which are Hellenistic), attached to symmetrical stanzas, originally indicated the turns and counter-turns of symmetrical dance patterns. This reminds us that, besides the music, we have lost the choreography, which was executed in figures of varying complexity. Conventions which today we would assign to ballet, opera, and oratorio are in Greek drama combined with a series of speaking parts to make something that we call by analogy a stage play, but which in fact is an ensemble uniquely Greek and classical and somewhat alien to modern expectations. It is a mistake, as any reader of *Agamemnon* or *Hippolytus* will discover, to think of plot as being restricted to the speaking parts. Lyric and dialogue are partners in the task of forwarding the action and exposing character and motive.

Though the place of performance of most but not all of these plays was the Theater of Dionysus on the southeast slope of the Acropolis and though one major occasion for the competition was the festival of the City Dionysia, this connection with the god and his cult—contrary to some widely held opinion—seems to have left no perceptible mark on the plays we have. *The Bacchae*, which might appear to be an exception, was not composed originally for performance in Athens, and its setting, we should note, is Theban. Even the Theater of Dionysus itself had replaced a more primitive arrangement in the market place. Furthermore tragic competitions were not restricted to the Dionysia. Latterly at least, they were also offered at the spring festival of the Lenaea. The link between Dionysus and the Greek theater became intimate in the Hellenistic age; their relationship in the sixth and fifth centuries is a matter of dispute, and was possibly somewhat fortuitous. Three prizes were awarded for first, second, and third places, and though special judges were selected for this purpose, they made their decision in front of the audience, which did not hesitate to register its own preferences. Thus the plays were composed for the Athenian public, not for an esoteric minority. Appeals to contemporary feeling on political and social issues are certainly not to be excluded on a priori grounds as violating the purity of Greek art. The reader himself will note without learned assistance how frequently a plot or episode manages to exploit Athenian pride and patriotism.

These original conditions of performance, as we have said, helped to mould the character of the text. The simplicity of the early playing area prompted the use of "verbal scenery" (instead of props and physical effects) and a "program" of plot and characters incorporated in the diction, most of it in the "prologue." But the plays were then revived continuously for centuries, during which time the details of staging, costumes, masks, the formal rules of dramaturgy, the profession of acting, and the construction of the theater itself, were all elaborated and formalized, even to some extent "modernized." The reader should be warned that in current handbooks on the subject he is likely to encounter much which draws on testimonies from these later periods, and which cannot be authenticated for the simpler but more creative conditions of the fifth century B.C.

E. A. H.

ON THE METRES OF GREEK TRAGEDY

One difference between Attic tragedy and opera is the domination of words over music. The music was there, in the choral passages, perhaps in all passages other than pure dialogue. But the rhythm of the words controlled the music. This is clearly to be inferred from the *strophic* structure of the full choral ode. A *strophe*, an elaborate series of metric elements arranged in a complex and unique pattern, will be followed by an *antistrophe* which repeats that pattern precisely, a long syllable in the one will match a long syllable in the other, and a short will match a short. This would be unthinkable as much in modern operatic forms as in medieval chant, where syllables can be lengthened or shortened, or can receive varying stress, as the rhythm of the music requires.

Greek metre depends on an alternation of long and short syllables, and not, as in English verse, on a sequence of stressed and unstressed syllables. In the main, there were three types of metre. First, in the dialogue, and in such passages as the spoken prologue and messengers' speeches, we have an iambic metre probably unaccompanied by music. It is called iambic trimeter because it can be best analyzed into three dipodies of two iambs each. There is a good analogy here with English blank verse, although the Greek line had six iambs rather than five as in English, and although the Greek line was stricter than the English analogue; in Greek comedy a good reader can instantly pick out a quoted or a parodied tragic trimeter from the surrounding comic trimeters by the greater regularity of the former. A typical line is 1. 12 of *Oedipus the King*:

ho pasi kleinos Oidipus kalumenos
the famous man whom all men know as Oedipus

where the single vertical represents the metrical division into dipodies, the double vertical the regular *caesura*, or word-ending within the third or fourth iambic foot.

When the chorus enter the orchestra in the *parodos*, again when they leave in the *exodos*, and in other passages, such as the introduction of new characters after a choral ode, the chorus, or one of the main characters, often speak in anapests. This metre can be arranged in lines, but in fact falls into *systems*, or long sequences, since there is no real metrical break at the end of the conventionally arranged lines. The series of anapests, that is, simply goes on until a shortened foot, a single syllable, coinciding with a verse-pause, ends the *system*. Thus we get ◡◡– ◡◡– . . . . . ◡◡– –. This is clearly a marching rhythm, and was usually accompanied by linear movement (on or off stage) by chorus or actors. Though some variations are allowed, spondees (– –) or dactyls (–◡◡) sometimes replacing the anapests (e.g., ◡◡– | – – | ◡◡– | –◡◡ | –◡◡–, etc. is possible), the anapestic is the steadiest, most driving, metre in Greek drama. Musically, it was probably between dialogue and choral song, probably accompanied by a simple melody and chanted rather than spoken, in a manner somewhat like *recitative*.

The full choral ode is an elaborate metrical, musical, and choreographic structure. In a modern English text, these odes often look like what used to be called *free verse*. They are in fact extremely tight structures, as the correspondence between strophe and antistrophe reveals. They are like free verse only in that each ode is a metrically unique creation: The metres are made up of known elements, but these elements are arranged into a pattern peculiar to the single ode.

The metrical structure of choral odes requires a book for adequate description. But three common types of metrical elements in them can be noted here. First *iambic*: here we have usually varied and syncopated iambic forms, appearing as short metrical cola, or sections; for example,

◡– ◡– | ʌ – ◡ – | ◡– ʌ –
◡– ◡– | ʌ – ◡ – | ◡– ʌ –

where the caret shows the missing syllable which would have made each
of the three parts of these two cola (appearing as *lines* in our text) a
standard iambic dipody. This metre is crisp and lively and relatively un-
complicated. In origin, it is closer to speech than other choral metres: In
the hands of Aeschylus, it could reach (as in the choral odes of *Agamemnon*) an unparalleled religious and dramatic solemnity.

The favorite choral metre of Sophocles was the Aeolic (so-called
because it appears in the lyric poetry of the Aeolic poets Sappho and
Alcaeus) composed of elements which appear to be expanded choriambs
(– ˘ ˘ –) with various combinations preceding and following them. The
most common element is the glyconic – ˘ – ˘ ˘ – ˘ –; but endless
variations are possible. It is perhaps the most mellifluous, and the most
capable of subtle modulation of all choral metres. Sometimes iambic
elements, and these sometimes in the form of a series of short syllables,
will be introduced with great dramatic effect in an Aeolic sequence; and
sometimes the Aeolic metre will be turned to the rapid and epic move-
ment of a dactylic sequence (– ˘ ˘ – ˘ ˘. . .). Both these variations occur, for example, in the great first stasimon of *Antigone* (332 f.).

The wildest and most eccentric metre is the *dochmiac*, which seems
to consist of staccato and abruptly syncopated iambic elements, typical
forms being ˘ – – ˘ – and ˘ ˘ ˘ ˘ ˘ ˘ –. This metre is used to mark statements of great fear or grief. The *parodos* of *The Seven Against Thebes*,
where the Theban women imagine their city taken, is an extended passage in dochmiacs. Another example is *Hippolytus*, 811 f., where the
chorus lament the suicide of Phaedra. Here as often in dochmiac, lines
of iambic trimeter, as in spoken dialogue, are interspersed (813, 819–28,
etc.). This may correspond to a break in the music and dancing, a further dramatic representation of extreme anxiety.

These choral or sung metres are most often uttered by the chorus,
but sometimes by a single character, in a monody, or more often, in a
lyric dialogue with the chorus. This latter is called a *kommos*, literally
(*self-*) *striking* or *lamentation*, because that is the usual mode of such
passages. By its nature, the kommos is often in dochmiac metre.

These are three of the principal metrical forms in choral song.
Each has its distinct *ethos*, or emotional tone; and this distinct emotion
was elaborated and enhanced by the dancing as well as the music, both
these parts of the overwhelming choral performance being composed so
as to correspond to the metrical pattern.

Sometimes more special metres are used in choruses for more special
effect, and we shall mention only two: (1) The chorus at the beginning
of *Agamemnon* as they move from their marching anapests into song

begin with a dactylic hexameter ‒◡◡ ‒◡◡ ‒◡◡ ‒◡◡ ‒◡◡ ‒ ‒, the metre of Homeric epic: that is clearly a deliberate recalling of the Homeric situation; (2) much of the *parodos* of *The Bacchae* (e.g., 64 ff.) is in an Ionic metre ◡◡‒ ‒ ◡◡‒ ‒, etc. That is because this metre was used in ritual hymns to Dionysus.

Finally, we should note the trochaic tetrameter ‒◡‒◡ ‒◡‒◡ ‒◡‒◡ ‒◡‒. A rapid and slightly rollicking form, this was said to be the original dialogue metre of tragedy, and its relative frequency in the early plays of Aeschylus may bear this out. It is a dialogue metre, is more formal than iambic trimeter, and expresses more hurry and agitation: e.g., *The Persians* 155–75, 215–48, where we note that for the Queen's long speech in 176–214, the metre reverts to the more conversational iambic trimeter.

The preceding is only a bare sketch of the intricacies, as well as the expressive possibilities, of Greek tragic metre. For fuller accounts (which, however, require some knowledge of Greek) see:

Oxford Classical Dictionary, article on *metre, Greek*, London: Oxford University Press, 1949.

D. S. Raven, *Greek Metre, an Introduction*, New York: Humanities Press, Inc., 1962.

W. J. W. Koster, *Traité de métrique grecque*, 2nd ed., Leiden: Brill, 1953.

ADAM PARRY

TRANSLATOR'S PREFACE

I have attempted, in the translation which follows, to render the text as closely as possible in something like "poetic" form. I have tried to maintain the iambic, six stress time and the trochaic tetrameter of the dialogue, as well as several of the passages of "recitative" anapests. For the lyric metres of the choral odes, I have attempted to preserve, not the original rhythms, but what my ear detected as the essential pattern, while also trying to suggest the close correspondence between matching stanzas.

The text is basically that of H. D. Broadhead (Cambridge, 1960), although I have sometimes followed the second Oxford edition of Murray-Maas (1955). The debt I owe to Broadhead's extensive and extremely helpful commentary will be obvious from the frequency with which it is cited in the notes. Also of use, particularly in matters of manuscript corruption and details of ritual and myth, is the *Commentary* of H. J. Rose (Amsterdam, 1957).

In annotating an edition like this, the translator is faced with the difficult decision of what to include, what to leave out. My principle has been to include as much as might help to elucidate some point raised by the text. By the very nature of the material, this information will be heavily historical. On the other hand, from the point of view of mode of expression and intended meaning, even the ancients found Aeschylus often obscure, even riddling, and matters are made worse by a grossly defective textual tradition (although *The Persians* is not so bad in this respect as, say, *Agamemnon*). It was therefore inevitable that some attention be paid in the notes to questions of language and text. At the same time, I hope I have paid enough attention also to such intrinsically more important matters as images and themes, points of staging and dramatic form, to assist the reader to an understanding of one of Aeschylus' most enigmatic but most profound dramas.

A. J. P.

THE PERSIANS

BY ÆSCHYLUS

INTRODUCTION

THE ACTION OF THE PLAY

The "action" of the play is briefly told. A Chorus composed of aged and venerable Persian councilors enters and sings of the greatest armament its land has ever sent forth, under the young King Xerxes, and with the object of conquering Greece. Against their transports of patriotic amazement at the splendor of the expedition is played a counterpoint of anxiety for the safety of these men sent so far from home and on so ambitious a venture; and, more than anxiety, a foreboding grows in intensity until it becomes almost an obsession (see lines 107 ff.) that the expedition may be an act of hybris, an attempt by mortal men and their youthful leader to escape the divinely imposed limitations of human finitude, and a venture, therefore, almost literally destined to miscarry. The Chorus' forebodings are reinforced by the Queen Mother, who comes from the palace to recount a dream, whose portentous import is also that Xerxes' attempt to yoke Greece to Asia is doomed to fail. Too true these intimations of disaster: a solitary Messenger, forerunner of the returning army, rushes breathlessly upon the scene to recount the utter defeat of the Persian hordes at Salamis; the hitherto matchless military grandeur of the Persian army was no match for Greek guile and the gods' antagonism, and but few are left from many. The Chorus,

1

in its song (532ff.), gives voice to all Asia's lament; the fabric of Persian rule must crumble. The Queen reappears with offerings to raise the ghost of her dead husband, the unvanquished Darius, and the Chorus conjures up his spirit with appropriate incantations. Darius appears, a specter from the vanished glories of the past, to learn of the disaster, to commiserate with his wife and suffering people, and to pinpoint responsibility for the defeat: Xerxes' youthful folly led him to devise a mad plan, but in doing so he was only falling in with the divinely ordained pattern; "whenever a man himself goes rushing in, God speeds him on" (742). Darius prophesies a further defeat at Plataea, and after a final ode in which the Chorus seeks escape in the remembered splendors of Darius' reign, the torn and battered Xerxes appears. The play ends with the defeated king and his councilors singing an antiphonal, almost ritualistic, lament for their fallen fortunes.

The Persians is Aeschylus' first surviving play, indeed the first extant Greek tragedy, and to readers who, like Aristotle, habitually measure all other Greek dramas by the standard of *Oedipus the King*, it must seem strange in many respects. For instance, what is the dramatic *action?* What really happens in the play? A messenger's speech, a ghost-raising, and the return of a defeated king: these are the sum total of external events. But let us shift our focus from action to dramatic *tension*. Against the glorious hopes, the wealth lavished on the expedition and its extravagant aims, stand the Chorus' fears, the Queen's unnerving dream, the Messenger's eyewitness tale of disaster, and, finally, Darius' prophecy of further sufferings. Against a backdrop of what Persia was and might have been, we see portrayed before us at the close the pathetic spectacle of what she has become, embodied in the dirty and disheveled king. Through the glorious drum-roll of names and nations that is the Chorus' entrance song runs an undercurrent of dread, the suggestions coming always more or less close to the surface that things are not what they seem. It is this polarity of voiced hope and unspoken but hinted fear that gives the opening scene the grip it undoubtedly holds on our attentions; and when the Queen enters to recount her dream, so painfully obvious in its import, we begin to move from suppressed to spoken fear for the army and the king, from uneasy hope of victory to creeping fear, and thence, with the Messenger's fatal news, to certainty of defeat. Through the vividness of the Messenger's eyewitness retelling of the encounter off Salamis, we become viewers of this most tragically decisive action, whereby Greeks and gods conjoined to ruin Persia's plans.

Looked at from one point of view, the action proper of the play is over, but the suffering and recognition of how deep and irremediable is the suffering remain. And throughout the play, from the first mention of his name in line 5, we, like the Persian elders and the Queen, await Xerxes. He it was who (in Aeschylus' rewriting of history, at least) conceived the plan, he who led forth the army and then allowed himself to be tricked by a Greek; it is his ignominious return to which the whole play is leading. In a sense, the ghost-raising scene is only a diversion, and the concern for the Persian nation, which apparently motivates the conjuring of Darius, is nothing more than the concentration of concern for Xerxes writ large. The Queen ill conceals that he is the focus of her interest (300–301, a concern shared by Darius, cf. 735); his father's Ghost is hardly on the scene when the dialogue is brought around to "furious Xerxes, who emptied out the whole broad-stretching continent" (718), and throughout the rest of their scene, mother and dead father analyze their son's actions.[1] Xerxes' appearance, in person, at the end should cause no surprise, even if the ritual litany of lament between defeated king and embittered subjects with which the play closes falls somewhat strangely on modern ears; for it is through this last antiphonal dirge, if anywhere, that the audience's emotions of fear and pity, aroused by the spectacle of the ruined king, would have achieved the purgation demanded by the Aristotelian theory.

---

[1] The concern of Darius and the Queen with providing Xerxes with suitable attire (833–36, 846–45) is best understood, I think, not as a clumsy attempt to get the Queen offstage, but rather as a tangible sign of the importance of the king's physical person.

INTRODUCTION

HISTORICAL TRAGEDY

Besides *The Persians* there is no other surviving ancient Greek drama (and only two titles, Phrynichus' *Sack of Miletus* and *The Phoenician Women*) on a theme from contemporary history. Unlike all other extant Greek tragedies, which deal with persons and events from the remote (we should say "mythical") past, *The Persians* is about living persons and events hardly eight years past when it was produced, in March 472 B.C. Its setting is Susa, the Persian capital; its hero, the Persian king who came so close to defeating the Greeks in 480 B.C.; its theme, his own defeat at their hands.

Aeschylus has done much to create an un-Greek atmosphere, with his catalogs of Eastern-sounding names, his heaping up of details and images that suggest strangeness and even exoticism, opulent wealth, and a concern with luxurious living; but to his audience (most of whom will have been men who themselves had fought the Persians scarcely eight years before), at the center of the play must have stood, undeniably, the fact of Xerxes' defeat and the converse fact of Greek victory. One may ask what else an Athenian writer could have done, but no creative writer has subjects forced upon him, and even historians can avoid topics they find uncongenial. Clearly Aeschylus chose a subject which he decided, for his own reasons, lent itself to tragedy. His success, the degree to which he attained his objective and stripped himself of a too-exclusively Athenian point of view, every reader must judge for himself. My own feeling is that he succeeded remarkably in creating a tragic action and, in Xerxes, a tragic sufferer, whom the audience would have seen, not as an enemy or as a Persian, but as a *man*, subject to the same turns of fortune as other men and victim of the same human condition. Darius, speaking for the poet, projects the action to a universal plane when he says, "man's condition means that sufferings will come to men" (706).

But the choice of subject imposed its own limitations. For one thing, to write a play about a near-contemporary event in which most of the audience would have been involved, if not as combatants at least as bystanders and near victims, required basic

4

fidelity to events as the Athenians remembered them. Slight variations of detail and shifts of emphasis were all that was allowed to Aeschylus; gross distortions of fact would not have been tolerated. In fact, as far as we can reconstruct a narrative of events from more strictly historical accounts like that of Herodotus, Aeschylus has presented a description of the antecedents and early stages of the battle of Salamis (353 and following) which deserves to be ranked as eyewitness reporting of a high order, and which Herodotus' narrative more than a generation later may be used to supplement but not correct.[2] But within the general framework of historical accuracy there has been some selection of detail and alteration of emphasis. A comparison with Herodotus' narrative shows that the contrast Aeschylus paints between the peace-loving, always successful, paternalistic Darius and the youthful, impetuous, almost mad, Xerxes (see, for example, 73, 718, 754; *thourios*, "furious," is a repeated epithet for Xerxes) has little basis in fact. That the son may appear the blacker, his father is painted in lighter tones. It is perhaps strictly true, if somewhat misleading, for the Chorus to describe Darius as "unharming" (555 and 663), for it means that Darius did not bring woes on his people, as Xerxes has done; but when the Chorus alludes to the cities Darius had captured "without ever crossing the Halys,/ Not even stirring from home" (865–66), we are entitled to remark that the king's abortive attempt to conquer the Scyths in about 514 B.C. seems conveniently forgotten.

The desire to heighten the contrast between father and son in two places plays the poet false in a more serious way. As an external sign of that insolent and overreaching attitude of mind which the Greeks called *hybris*, Xerxes' bridging of the Hellespont is several times alluded to. Darius quite naturally wonders how so huge a land army was transported across to Europe. "Cunningly he yoked the strait of Helle [that is, the Hellespont] so it held a road" (722), the Queen replies, and Darius exclaims in horror, "Some powerful Spirit must have come to take away his wits"

---

[2] For details, see Appendix A of my study, *The Political Background of Aeschylean Tragedy* (Ann Arbor: University of Michigan Press, 1966), pp. 131ff.

(725). Darius clearly implies that for his son to have dared such a deed was the highest sacrilege. Later in the same scene (745–48) Darius expands upon the theme:

> [Xerxes] who hoped to check the flow of sacred Hellespont with bonds,
> Shackled like some slave the Bosporus, the holy spring of God.
> Forcing his route to take a shape against its nature and casting on
> Hammered chains, he managed to make a road to match his mass of men.

The implication throughout the scene is obvious: "How different I was!" But this is highly misleading, not to say false, for we learn from Herodotus (4. 83) that Darius himself performed a similar feat when he bridged the Thracian Bosporus preparatory to his invasion of Scythia. Aeschylus may not have known about Darius' bridge, but the same excuse can hardly be offered for a detail he seems to have invented sheerly for the sake of the contrast we have been discussing. Darius introduces, somewhat cryptically, a reference to the "instructions" he says his son had forgotten (782–83). The content of these instructions is left to the audience's imagination, but the implication is clear that Xerxes, in attacking Greece, has done something which his father had specifically forbidden. Not only do we hear nothing of this in any other source, but what evidence we have points precisely to an opposite conclusion. According to Herodotus, after the failure of the first invasion at Marathon in 490 B.C., Darius was even more eager to add Greece to the Persian dominions. For three years he enlisted a new and larger force, "selecting and equipping the choicest troops for the invasion" (Herodotus 7. 1); only death prevented him from carrying out his plan. When Xerxes succeeded his father, "he was not at all eager at first to march against Greece" (7. 5), and it took a great deal of prompting from several quarters to set him in his purpose. Aeschylus' picture is quite different: that of a young hothead, goaded into trying to surpass his father's achievement and anxious not to be called a cowardly stay-at-home (753 and following). We can see what the poet is

6

doing for his own dramatic purposes, and we must reluctantly agree with Broadhead's comment on 753, that Darius' strictures on his son are sheer fabrication.

One final shift of focus by the poet deserves notice. History records the campaign of 480–479 as having been won in three separate battles (Salamis in the fall of 480, and Plataea and Mycale the following summer), but for Aeschylus, "the defeat of Xerxes was Salamis, and the victor was Athens." [3] Salamis echoes through the tragedy, either by name (see 272, 284, 965) or in allusions unmistakable to Athenian ears (303, 307, 309, 390, 570, 595, 894–96, 954). Marathon is merely mentioned (475), and Plataea is relegated to second place (805ff.).

What can have been Aeschylus' reason for this historical compression, this concentration of the whole Greek resistance into one engagement? If the Spartans could claim Plataea, Salamis was uniquely an Athenian victory, and more than that, uniquely Themistocles'. When the Messenger begins his account of the battle with the words ". . . a man, a Greek, arrived from the Athenian camp / And spoke to your son Xerxes . . ." and then proceeds to recount details of the lying message by which Themistocles had achieved his *coup de théâtre* (355 and following), every member of the original audience knew that it was Themistocles who was meant. Aeschylus comes as close to naming a contemporary Greek political figure as the conventions of the Athenian stage allow, and he concentrates all our attention on Themistocles himself by removing from the story, or conveniently forgetting about, the slave Sicinnus—whom, according to Herodotus, Themistocles had used to carry his message to Xerxes. Using every dramatic device at his disposal, Aeschylus is doing his best to remind his audience of Themistocles' part in the victory against Persia. Why? Fortunately, the date of the play, spring 472 B.C., is certain; and although the sources are less precise about the chronology of Themistocles' career, we know that about this time his own political fortunes and personal popularity had waned to the extent that he was struck down with two legal penalties

---

[3] Richmond Lattimore, "Aeschylus on the Defeat of Xerxes," *Classical Studies in Honor of William Abbott Oldfather* (Urbana: University of Illinois, 1943), p. 93.

7

which no politician could survive: first ostracism, a relatively honorable device by which a man was removed from Athens for ten years, and then *atimia*, outlawry, or in effect, condemnation as a public enemy, which entailed confiscation of a man's property and even exposed his immediate family to the dangers of prosecution. We know that Themistocles was thus penalized, but we have no way of knowing exactly when, and it is impossible to try to date his exile and condemnation from the known date of *The Persians*. This much, however, is clear: Aeschylus is taking a stand for Themistocles when the latter's fortunes were at their lowest ebb, perhaps, as some have thought, in the months preceding his ostracism, when his enemies at Athens began to gather their "evidence" and muster public opinion against him. Aeschylus chose, at that critical time in Themistocles' life, to write a tragedy on a theme which cannot have failed to remind the audience of its debt to Themistocles' personal cunning and strategic skill; the poet placed at the center of his Messenger-account of the defeat a passage in which dramatic attention is focused wholly on Themistocles, and Themistocles himself is all but named. It takes nothing from the dramatic excellence of the play or from the powerful conception of Xerxes as a tragic sufferer to admit that Aeschylus might have had an extrinsic motive for writing this play, on just this theme, at just this time: a personal attachment to Themistocles, and a desire to recall the Athenians from the ungrateful and shortsighted course they had embarked on.[4]

THE PRODUCTION; POSSIBLE ANTECEDENTS

An inscription which gives a list of annual winners in the dramatic competitions contains the information that in this year, in which a certain Menon was chief magistrate at Athens (472 B.C.), Aeschylus won first prize for tragedy and that his *chorēgus*, or producer, was Pericles. We have no further information than that, but several interesting theories might result from speculations about why the great statesman-to-be, whose first public act

---

[4] I have argued the case more fully in *The Political Background of Aeschylean Tragedy*, Chapter II.

this is of which we have any record and who could have been hardly more than twenty years old, chose to put his financial backing behind a play in support of Themistocles. The play itself was second in a tetralogy consisting of *Phineus, The Persians, Glaucus Potneius,* and—a rather surprising topic for the rough humor of a satyr-play—*Prometheus.* Little enough remains of the other plays, and what there is—or what can be reconstructed on the basis of the myths with which they deal—suggests that the poet did not here follow the practice, which he himself may have introduced into the composition of Greek tragedy, of elaborating successive stages of a single story and providing a thematic, if not also a chronological, connection from one play to another within the trilogy. The only complete surviving Aeschylean trilogy, the *Oresteia,* will serve as an example, but there were others: the Theban trilogy, which dealt with the Laius-Oedipus story, of which only the third play, *The Seven Against Thebes,* survives; and the Danaid trilogy, whose first play, *The Suppliants,* is extant. As far as the poor shreds of *Phineus* that remain show anything at all, the play probably retold the story of the blind prophet-king of Thrace, whose mealtimes were harassed by those bird-women called Harpies, and who, in return for showing Jason and his Argonauts the way to Colchis and its golden fleece, was rewarded by being rid of the Harpies by Calais and Zetes, the sons of Boreas. Rather more remains of *Glaucus* ("of Potniae," a town near Thebes in Boeotia, to distinguish it from *The Marine Glaucus,* apparently an Aeschylean satyr-play). Glaucus, son of the unhappy Sisyphus, who had succeeded to the throne of Ephyra (later Corinth), entered the chariot race in the funeral games honoring Pelias, but was devoured by his own mares, for what reason we cannot tell; but Glaucus clearly has certain affinities with Lycurgus, Pentheus, and Hippolytus, mortals destroyed for refusing worship to some divinity. According to one version of the story, Aphrodite was angered by Glaucus' refusal to allow his mares to couple with stallions before the race in order to increase their speed.

There is no obvious thematic relation among the plays of the trilogy. Broadhead (*Intro.,* lv–lx) discusses some attempts to create one, but we must admit that as far as we can tell in the

9

present state of the evidence, *The Persians*, with its historical theme, is *sui generis*, not only in its trilogy but in the whole Aeschylean corpus.

The above-mentioned inscription proves that *The Persians* was presented at Athens and guarantees its date, but there are two additional ancient references to a production (and one of them says a re-production) in Syracuse, at the eager request of the Sicilian tyrant, Hiero. Aeschylus' connections with Hiero are confirmed by other references, and a second production of the play in Sicily (presumably at some date after its Athenian première) is not at all unlikely. All the same, there is no good evidence that this was a substantially different version of the play, and the theory of a "Sicilian text," which seems to have originated in the second century B.C., remains unproved. That further evidence, perhaps in the papyri, may yet appear to confirm it, is an open, if remote, possibility.[5]

A more serious problem is raised by the reference, in the *Ancient Prefatory Note* to the play (see page 20 of this translation), to Aeschylus' alleged "adaptation" from his predecessor Phrynichus. What is it that Aeschylus can have adapted? The writer, or compiler, of the *Note* quotes the first line of Phrynichus' *The Phoenician Women*, Aeschylus' alleged model, and it is so much like the opening of *The Persians* as to suggest that there may have been other verbal similarities between the two plays. But verbal echoes, although they are interesting and indicate how little the ancient Greeks were troubled by copying so close that we would call it "plagiarism," are much less important than the implicit identity of theme between the two plays. Phrynichus' *The Phoenician Women*, whose title is derived from the chorus' composition (wives of the men in the Phoenician contingents who made up the bulk of Xerxes' naval crews), almost certainly also focused on the victory of Salamis. As only some half-dozen fragmentary lines survive, this last point cannot be asserted with complete confidence, but that a battle in which Greeks won over Per-

---

[5] The evidence is presented and discussed at length by Broadhead in his *Introduction*, xlviii *sqq.*, with a judicious *non liquet* at li. (I have gone into this matter in greater detail in the "Appendix," pp. 117 ff.)

sians was recounted at length by a messenger seems beyond doubt; and although some scholars believe other battles were involved (for example, that off Cape Mycale[6] in Ionia in early fall 479), a piece of circumstantial evidence seems to me to rule out any but Salamis. We know from Plutarch that Themistocles himself served as *chorēgus* for Phrynichus in 476 B.C., and although the play is not named, it is an all but inescapable inference (made first by the British scholar Richard Bentley in the eighteenth century) that it was Phrynichus' *The Phoenician Women*. What could be more likely than that at this time, when perhaps Themistocles' popularity had already begun to slip, the poet who is known to have composed at least one other historical tragedy and the hero of Salamis should have allied to remind the Athenians of that battle's importance to the national survival of Greece, and also of Themistocles' responsibility for the victory? In other words, it seems to me in the highest degree likely that in 472 B.C., Aeschylus chose as his model and inspiration a work which had been presented four years earlier and which could almost be said to have been "commissioned" by Themistocles. So far from being fortuitous, the verbal borrowings were probably, then, intended by Aeschylus to reinforce the basic similarity of theme and treatment between his own and his predecessor's play, and the political "message" of the two plays will likewise have been the same.

LEVELS OF TRAGIC ACTION; GODS AND MEN

As elsewhere in Aeschylean tragedy, the action works itself out on several levels at the same time. The most obvious, perhaps, is the *national* one: the Persian army made its expedition to subjugate Greece as a nation; the failure of the attempt is a national disaster, for Persia as a nation no longer exists (714, 752). The army's wealthy trappings, all gilded luxury, are repeatedly emphasized (3, 9, 37, 53, 79, etc.); this is the national wealth for which the Queen expresses such solicitude, wealth that has gone into building an army which the world considered invincible (27–

---

[6] The view that Mycale was the battle featured by Phrynichus is convincingly refuted by Giuseppe Nenci in *Parola del Passato* 5 (1950) 216 note 1.

28, 87ff.). Again and again we are told that all the men, the entire strength of Asia, have gone forth (12, 42, 61); the cities of Persia are depopulated, empty (119, 549, 718, 730, 761), and, after the disaster, will never be filled again. The young men, whom the earth herself nurtured (62, 512, 922–23, 925) are gone and will not return to recompense their mother with support in old age. "And the land of Asia," as the Chorus sings at the end, "has terribly, terribly sunk to her knees" (929–30). The nation feels the disaster not only materially and physically, in loss of wealth and men, but also *politically*. Her great dominions, control over her subject peoples, are now in danger: the great honor which mastery gave is gone (762, 919); no longer will Persia impose her laws as the laws of her subjects (585, 919; cf. 95ff.).

On a more intimate level, the tragedy is a *domestic* one, a family affair. The Queen, in her opening scene, in lines which have struck most commentators as obscure, voices a fear that "Riches . . . may trample down . . . prosperity" (163–64), the prosperity that Darius won "not without one of the gods." "A single stroke has brought about the ruin of great Prosperity" says the Messenger in his opening lines (251–52), where the wealth of the royal family is surely counted as part of the national prosperity that has perished. The Queen alludes again later to the prosperity Darius had accumulated (709), and she gives a solution to her enigmatic opening lines. Xerxes was driven to prove his mettle by nagging critical tongues who maintained that Darius had acquired great wealth for his sons, whereas his heir Xerxes was doing nothing to increase his inherited prosperity (755–56). This wealth of the royal house has now been overturned (751–52; cf. 163); through overreaching, Xerxes has "spill[ed] a store of great prosperity" (826). We see the tragedy, too, as one in which the characters of the play are intimately concerned as members of a *family*. The Queen's first words are of her husband (160). She soon relates a dream in which both son and husband figure, both of them in typical, erring-son, warning-father, roles (197–98). After she reports her dream, the Chorus addresses her as "mother" (215)—for this is her primary function in the play—in much the same filial way that they will later call Darius "father" (663, 671). Mention of her son is never far from the Queen's lips (211, 227, 353, 473,

12

476, and throughout). She sees the tragedy through the eyes of other parents who have lost their sons in the war (245); her own son's safety brings light even in darkness (300–301). As she leaves the stage, she urges the Chorus to comfort him and escort him home (530). Her offerings are brought to Darius' shade as "my son's father" (609).

In the great scene with Darius, the Queen and dead King discuss Xerxes' expedition very much as if it were a family affair. Which son was it, Darius asks, who led the expedition (717)? He must have been out of his mind (725, 744, 749). And, as we have seen, Xerxes turns out (somewhat surprisingly; it is a new motif) to have led the army to Greece precisely to surpass the glorious achievements of his father (754–58). In fatherly tones, Darius castigates Xerxes' youth, his young and foolish schemes (782), his failure to heed parental advice (783). In echo of one of the Queen's earlier lines, he now urges her, as "Xerxes' aged mother," to provide Xerxes with suitable attire to replace the robes he tore at Salamis (832ff.). At least she can do this, a symbolic saving of her son's tattered dignity and prestige (846 with note). And, unless I have overinterpreted, there are several hints that even the succession may be in danger because of Xerxes' defeat; there seems to be a real possibility that the royal house may fall. Much of its personal fortune must have gone to equipping the army—could the "national wealth" and the family fortune even have been distinguished?—and the "ancestral wealth" is, as we saw, now considered lost. The Queen had expressed a fear that "Men who lose their wealth have not the radiant strength that once they had" (167). In breaking off her speech to point out that Xerxes "owes the city no explanations" (213), she protests too much and raises our suspicions. As the Chorus ominously remarks, ". . . the mass of men / Went loose and free in their speech / When the yoke of [royal] strength was loosened" (592–94). The old men of the Chorus themselves even exercise some of this new freedom as they bitterly reproach the battered and defeated king. *Stasis*, revolution, is one of the first things to come to the Ghost's mind when he hears that there is trouble (715). The Queen expresses a fear of some "further harm" (531), and although a threat to the throne is not explicitly meant, it is not excluded either (see note on 531).

Finally, *The Persians* is also a tragedy of one man, young and foolish, perhaps, but basically noble and even well intentioned; Xerxes, in fact, is a character who comes closer than anyone else in Aeschylus to the usual conception of a "tragic hero," a man who, in his grand designs, attempts to scale the heights of heaven and falls to his doom. "Hybris" and "godless thoughts" are specifically ascribed to him by his father (808, cf. 821). His designs are overbearing (827–28), and he is charged with "wounding God with overboastful rashness" (831; cf. 744). His fault is primarily one of ignorance, a failure of intelligence—and that is the basic meaning of *harmartia* (Aristotle's word, the word the Chorus uses at 676): his wits were taken away (725), and he acted "blindly" (744). More precisely, "Mortal that he was he foolishly thought that he could master all / Gods . . . some disease of mind" (749–50). The moral of Xerxes' story is that "mortal man should not think more than mortal thoughts" (820).

If this were all there was to the play, we might have an Aristotelian tragedy, but we would not have an Aeschylean one. For Aeschylus adds another dimension, the divine or *demonic*. We forgive Xerxes, even sympathize with him, not only for his youth and ignorance, but also—and mainly—because he was in a real sense driven to disaster by some power outside his control. "But what mortal can escape God's crafty snare?" the Chorus asks in the entrance song; "Man is coaxed in seeming goodwill / To the net of ruin" (107–8, 111–12). "Some powerful Spirit must have come to take away his wits," says Darius (725). In the last words of the entrance song, the Chorus suggests ominously that "their ancient lucky fortune," the ancient spirit of good luck (*daimōn*), may have abandoned them (158). In its place there is a new Spirit of Destruction, which dominates the play. "Some Spirit [*daimōn*] crushed the host," says the Messenger (345), and he begins his account of the battle of Salamis by telling how "Some Curse or Evil Spirit . . . appeared from somewhere" (354). This hateful spirit is addressed repeatedly throughout the play (472 and 845 by the Queen, 515 by the Chorus); the word *daimōn*, for which the nearest English equivalent is "Spirit," occurs some twenty times in all. Its hostile action is directed, not only against Xerxes personally, but against the whole Persian nation; several times it is said to have "leaped on" the Persians, giving them a wrestler's flying kick (516, 911), or to have mown them down like a reaper (921). When Xerxes appears he changes the figure: the *daimōn* has "veered / And now turned his blast on me" (942–43).

Occasionally, the word is used simply as an equivalent for "fortune" or "lot" (601, 602, 825), but in general it stands for a specific, almost personal, agency, which stalks the house and race. Particularly significant are the occurrences in which the term is applied to Darius: he is a king equal to a *daimōn* (633) or, simply, a *daimōn* (620, 640). We are meant to believe that there is something more than human about the former king, not only now that he is dead and "blessed," but even in life. The Chorus calls the Queen "Consort of the God of Persians, mother also of their God" (157). Darius' wealth was won "with help from one of the gods" (164). In the invocation scene, the Chorus prays to the nether powers to release the "God born in Susa" (643), who was "God's counselor" for them (654, 655). When Darius appears, the Queen reminds him that he had led his life "successfully among the Persians, like a God" (711). There are even hints that the poet intended the dead king to *embody* the *daimōn* of the royal house: when he was alive, all went well, wealth poured in, effortless conquests were made; now, with his death, the *daimōn* has changed (158), veered (942). It is almost as if the house (and the race) had lost its Guardian Spirit.

With the departure of this charm against evil, the divine plan works itself out against the Persians and in favor of the Greeks. It had been "God's divine order / Long ago decreed" that the Persian race should conquer (93–94); this was an honor which Zeus himself had bestowed (762). Now, "the gods are keeping the Goddess Pallas' city safe" (347); "God / Gave glory in the naval battle to the Greeks" (454–55). Divine warnings were also given. The Ghost reveals, somewhat to our surprise, that "the gods' prophetic statements" had foretold the ruin of Persia's might (800–801), but he had thought the gods would fulfill them only at some long distant date (741). It was part of Xerxes' folly, his blind infatuation (Atē, 822; cf. 653 and 1007), that he did not see that he was falling into the trap, fitting into the divine plan by his own free agency. Xerxes acted "not comprehending / The

15

treachery of the Greek, the jealousy of the gods," says the Messenger (361–62)—the divine and human levels intersect—and "He did not know what was about to come from the gods" (373). Even at the end Xerxes protests his ignorance: His fate "gave no sign" (910); his suffering was "unforeseen" (1028).

The Chorus had called the Persians' sufferings *daimonic* (581), heaven-sent (573); "God has turned it around" (905; cf. 943), but the fault and the tragedy are in no way any less Xerxes' own thereby. For, in a line which can be taken as a capsule summary of the play, "whenever a man himself goes rushing in, God speeds him on" (742), and "some Spirit aided in his plan" (724). It was none the less *his* for its being divinely foretold and even predetermined. This is the paradox, the mystery, of Aeschylean tragedy (we might say, of life): man loses none of his responsibility, even though God, for His part, surrenders none of His control.

METRICAL SCHEMA

1–149 This is the *Parodos*, or entrance song. The rhythm to 64 is *anapestic dimeter* (two units of two anapests, ⌣⌣‒, with frequent substitution of two shorts for one long and vice versa; the usual concluding cadence is called a "paroemiac" and contains ⌣⌣‒‒ in the second member). It is a marching beat, which would have been chanted by the members of the Chorus as they entered through the righthand side entrance (also *parodos*). Lines 65–139 are composed of six matching pairs of lyrical stanzas, or *strophai*, composed of more complicated rhythms (ionics, ⌣⌣‒‒, to 114; chiefly trochaic thereafter); the Chorus not only sang the words to musical accompaniment, it reinforced the close metrical correspondence between the matching stanzas with carefully balanced dance movements. At 140, it returns to anapests (likewise the metre announcing the Queen's arrival at 150–54).

16

155–175   The metre now changes to trochaic ($-\smile$) tetrameter, difficult to catch in English and now slightly antique sounding. Aristotle (*Poetics* 4. 14) maintained that it was the primitive metre of drama before the more natural iambic predominated, and the large proportion of trochaic lines in this, the first extant Greek tragedy, may bear him out.

176–214   The Queen speaks in iambic trimeters (three units of two iambi, or the equivalent), the metre which was to become the standard vehicle for dramatic dialogue. As Aristotle remarked in the *Poetics* (4. 14), it is very close to the rhythms of natural speech.

215–248   The metre changes back to trochaic tetrameter for the remaining dialogue.

256–289   The Chorus sings lyric iambics in paired stanzas; the Messenger's iambic trimeters are spoken.

532–597   This is the first song, or *stasimon*, of the Chorus after its entrance song and the short lament, in which the Messenger joins at 256–89. Somewhat unusually, the paired stanzas are prefaced by a series of anapests (532–47), as in the parodos; this seems to have been characteristic of early tragedy.

598–632   These lines are in iambic trimeter, followed by an anapestic prelude (623–32) to the ode that follows.

633–680   "The climax of the action is approaching and the tense excitement of the Chorus with its piteous appeals coupled with groanings and cries of despair is well brought out by the variety of the appropriate metres, in particular the choriambic, the ionic and the dochmiac" (Broadhead).

681–758   Darius begins his speech in iambics, but after a short choral *strophe* (694–96; *antistrophe*, 700–702), resumes in trochaic tetrameters.

759–851   The metre changes back to iambics.

17

852–1076 The play ends in totally lyric metres. The third *stasimon* (852–906) is composed of dactyls, with trochaic elements, a combination that gives a "stately effect" (A. M. Dale). From 907 to the end, Xerxes and the Chorus sing alternatingly, first in stanzaic pattern and then in single lines of "lyric" *stichomythia.*

This type of lyric scene, to which various technical names (such as *kommos* or *thrēnos*) were applied in antiquity, seems to have had ancient roots in the dirges, or laments, sung by the common people at least as early as the Homeric period.

ANCIENT PREFATORY NOTE

Glaucus in his work on "The Poetry of Aeschylus" says that *The Persians* was copied from *The Phoenician Women* of Phrynichus. He also quotes the beginning of the latter play as follows:

These belong to the Persians, long since gone. . . .

The difference is that in Phrynichus' play it is a eunuch who announces the defeat of Xerxes at the beginning, and arranges seats for the magistrates' assistants. In this play a chorus of elders delivers the prologue; the setting of the drama is near Darius' tomb. The plot is as follows: Xerxes led an expedition against Greece with a great armament, at the head of numberless cavalry, and a fleet of 1,207. After the infantry was defeated at Plataea, and the navy at Salamis, he fled through Thessaly and crossed over into Asia.

Aeschylus entered the tragic competition in the archonship of Menon (472 B.C.) and won the victory with *Phineus, The Persians, Glaucus Potnieus,* and *Prometheus.*

The first onslaught of the Persians in the time of Darius came to grief at Marathon; the second, that of Xerxes, at Salamis and Plataea.

19

ANCIENT PREFATORY NOTE

These ancient "Prefatory Notes" are probably a late compilation from various sources, one of them almost certainly the energetic librarians in Hellenistic Alexandria. Who this Glaucus was has been disputed: he is probably the Glaucus who wrote towards the end of the fifth century B.C. at Rhegium in Italy, and was thus one of the earliest Greek literary critics.

A fragment of an inscription (*I.G.* ii.^{2} 2318), which seems to have been the official record of the Athenian dramatic competitions, confirms that Aeschylus presented his plays in the archonship of Menon (473/2 B.C.; the plays would have been performed at the Great Dionysia in the spring of 472) and adds the detail that his producer was Pericles of the deme Cholargus. For a discussion of what is known about the other plays in the trilogy, see above, pages 9–10.

CHARACTERS *

CHORUS of old men

DARIUS' Ghost

MESSENGER

ATOSSA

XERXES

---

* This is almost certainly a later addition to the author's original manuscript; some modern editors print "Atossa" in their texts, but as her name is never used by any of the other characters, and the original audience would have had no programs, I have preferred to designate her simply "Queen." Similarly, in the text of the play Darius is never called "Ghost," *eidōlon* (although he seems to be referred to as a *psychē* at 630), and *eidōla* in Homer and elsewhere normally speak only in dreams. So it is possible that the stage direction which precedes 681 should read simply *Darius*, as also here. The identification of the character "Clytemnestra's Ghost" in the manuscripts of Aeschylus' *The Eumenides* is exactly similar. This kind of literal-minded erudition characterizes the later scholarly (or school-masterly) comments which frequently worked their way into the text.

22

THE PERSIANS

Scene: The play is set in Susa. The permanent scene-front represents a building whose nature cannot now be determined; a separate structure representing DARIUS' tomb may also have been present. A CHORUS of elderly men, probably twelve in number, enters by the righthand side entrance, or *parodos*; they are dressed in suitably rich and exotic-looking robes, perhaps over the patterned trousers of the type worn by Asiatics on Greek vases. They chant the opening lines as they enter.

CHORUS   *We are the ones whom the Persians gone*
To the land of Greece left behind

That the action occurs in Susa is proved by lines 118–19 (other references to the city at 15 and 511, with "Susa and Ecbatana" as a kind of formula to include the whole Persian empire at 16 and 535). What the building that served as a backdrop is intended to represent must remain a mystery; see note on 141, "this ancient abode."

1   The line ends with the ominous word *oichomenōn*, which occurs again at 13, with echoes at 60, 252, 546, and 916. To a Greek it would have suggested "gone forever," "dead and gone."

23

And entitled trustees of their rich
Estates laden with gold. Our years
Made Lord Xerxes, King,   5
Son of Darius,
     Choose us to watch over the land.

When I think of the King's
And the gold-laden army's return,
My heart, prophetic of doom,   10
Is troubled within me.
For all of Asia's strength
Has gone off behind its young master;

3–   rich . . . gold strikes one of the keynotes of the play: the
4   enormous wealth of the Persian nation which has gone into
     the expedition against Greece. The single Greek word here
     translated "laden with gold" (poluchrusos) recurs at 9, 45,
     and 53.

5–   Xerxes: pronounce Zerk'-sēz.
6   The king's formal titles are recited with ceremonial ful-
     someness. It is an authentic touch, as is shown from the title
     "King of Kings" on the autobiographical inscription in three
     languages—Persian, Elamite, and Akkadian—which DARIUS
     had set up at Behistun in 520 B.C. to commemorate his seizure
     of power and the victories by which he solidified his control
     at the beginning of his reign (A. T. Olmstead, History of
     the Persian Empire [Chicago, 1948] 116–18). The litany of
     titles measures the distance between the king and these, his
     loyal servants.

9   Herodotus (9. 80) catalogues the spoils taken from the Per-
     sians after the battle of Plataea as including "tents fitted with
     gold . . . gilded chairs . . . golden bowls . . . gold dag-
     gers."

10   Once again, an ominous note is sounded. In a similar image,
     the chorus in Aeschylus' Agamemnon describes the "attend-
     ant fear fluttering about the clairvoyant heart" (976–77).

13   Has gone at the beginning recalls and reinforces the last
     word of the opening line. For the remainder of the line no

But no courier, no rider comes
To the Persians' citadel.   15

These men set out from Susa, Ecbatana
And the ancient walled city of Cissia;
Left their land behind and went,
On horse, on ship, on foot,
    A solid column of war.   20
Men like Amistres and Artaphrenes
And Megabates and Astaspes,
Marshals of the Persians,

---

convincing interpretation or satisfactory emendation has
been suggested.

15 Clearly a reference to Susa, the scene of the play; see 118–19.

16– With the general effect of this passage compare Herodotus'
64 description of XERXES' reviewing his army (7. 60–97).

16 *Susa:* mentioned first as XERXES' capital, was in the western
part of the Persian empire.

Ecbatana: capital of the old empire of the Medes, the
most important city in the east.

17 *Cissia:* pronounce *Kiss'-ēa:* A separate third city, Cissia,
seems to be intended, although the name is used by Herodotus (5. 49) for the district in which Susa was located.

21– To what extent do these and later catalogs (e.g., 302–28,
22 958–99) represent actual historical personages among the
Persian commanders, men whose names members of the
audience might even have recognized? The question cannot
be answered with certainty. Attempts have been made to
identify certain of these names with individuals mentioned
by Herodotus (e.g., Artaphrenes), and Aeschylus may have
picked up some bits of authentic fact in this regard; it seems
unlikely, however, that he is trying to be completely authentic. It is the flavor of names that sound strange and yet are
recognizably Persian that gives these catalogs their intended
effect. (See Broadhead's *Appendix* V, pp. 318–21.)

Kings, the Great King's servants,
Surge forward, overseers of a great host,   25
Archers and horsemen
Fearful to behold, dreadful in battle
    For repute of their steadfast courage.
Artembares, fighter from steeds,
And Masistes and the archer   30
Noble Himaeus, and Pharandares
And driver of horses, Sosthenes.
Others by the great and fructifying
Nile were sent: Sousiskanes,
Pegastagon born in Egypt,   35
And the ruler of sacred Memphis,
Great Arsames, and regent of
Wealthy Thebes, Ariomardos,
And marsh-dwelling rowers of ships,
Skilled and in numbers above counting.   40

In their train was a throng of Lydians,
Lovers of luxury, who control the entire
Mainland race, those whom Mitrogathes,

---

24   Once again, scholars have detected an echo of the Behistun
     inscription (see note on 5–6).

39   Thucydides (1. 110) remarks that these marsh-dwellers in
     the Nile Delta were considered "the most warlike of the
     Egyptians." The Egyptians contributed two hundred ships
     to the Persian fleet (Herodotus 7. 89).

40   Anarithmoi, "innumerable," is followed shortly by "luxu-
     rious-lived" in 42: the two dominant themes are found, so to
     speak, back to back.

42– In saying that the Lydians "control" the entire (Asiatic)
43   mainland race (which would have included the Ionians),
     Aeschylus may be making subtle excuses for the Ionians,
     whom the Athenians looked upon as their colonists and
     descendants but who were on the wrong side in the Persian
     Wars (see notes on 178, 950ff., and 1025); "they were held

And noble Arkteus, lieutenant princes,
Sent speeding from golden Sardis 45
In numberless chariots,
Squadrons two and three abreast,
 A fearful sight to behold.
The neighbors of Tmolus' sacred height vow
To cast upon Greece their enslaving yoke: 50
Mardon, Tharybis, those anvils of the spear,
And Mysian javeliners. Babylon, too,
Rich in gold, sends a motley throng,
A long line of men who sail upon ships
Or trust in the tight temper of the bow. 55
And the spear-bearing mass from all
Asia follows,
 A dread escort to the King.

Such youthful bloom of men from the Persian

---

down by force," he may be saying, ("but would have revolted if they had been able").

49 Mt. Tmolus is near Sardis.

51 The first of many Aeschylean images whose exact meaning cannot—and need not—be specified; too literal an interpretation would have these men the recipients of spear-blows (as an anvil is struck by the hammer). Although this meaning is possible—for the spear elsewhere in the play can be symbolic of Greek strength in war—the phrase suggests rather that the Persian warriors must be anvil-hard, and their tough strength manifests itself in the spear, a parallel to the javelin-throwers of the next line.

52 The Mysians, a once independent people, were located in northwest Asia Minor. They are catalogued by Herodotus (7. 74), along with the Lydians, as a contingent in XERXES' army under the command of Artaphrenes (cf. 21).

55 The line recalls, but expands upon, Homer's "trusting in bows" (The Iliad 5. 105).

59 This metaphor, which becomes somewhat stereotyped in later literature, recurs at 252 and 925.

27

Land has gone;   60
For them the whole Asian Earth,
Their Mother, is consumed with grief
And longing. Parents and wives stretch out
The numbered days, and are afraid.

STROPHE 1

Across have the Persian city-sackers gone,   65
The royal army,
To the opposite neighboring shore,

61– The land mourning for her sons who have gone to defend
62 her is a time-worn theme; its freshness and vigor here are
    enhanced by the careful construction of 62: "having nursed
    them, in longing mourns, an all-consuming [longing]," where
    the climactic adjective (*maleros*) bears Homeric overtones
    connected with fire; to connect it with *pothos* (longing) is a
    bold conjunction, unparalleled, as far as I am aware, in
    other poets.

63– The anapestic introduction ends with the touching picture
64 of those left behind.

65– The themes introduced in the first section, the size and
139 splendor of the expedition, are here recapitulated with greater
    emotional intensity, and the tone of dread and foreboding,
    only hinted at before, rises to a dominant pitch.

65 *city-sackers:* a pun, for the first half of the compound not
    only means "sacking," but suggests "Persians." The audience
    probably thought of the sack of Athens in 480. If proof were
    needed of the impact this line made on the audience, an
    ancient commentator quotes a prose parody of it by the
    comic poet Eupolis some fifty years later.

68 *neighboring:* Built into this deceptively simple word is the
    whole long history of border feuds between coterminous
    states, enlarged now to a cosmic scale.

Crossing Helle's strait   70
On a bolted road of flax-bound rafts,
Throwing a yoke on the neck of the sea.

ANTISTROPHE 1

The furious lord of teeming Asia rages
Over every land,
Driving his splendid herds,   75
Attacking on foot and by sea,
Trusting his marshals strong and true,
Of golden race, a godlike man.   80

STROPHE 2

Casting a dark glare from his eyes,

70– The Hellespont was named for Helle (or Hella), daughter of
71 Athamas. According to Herodotus (7. 36) the boats (or
"rafts," as Aeschylus styles them) were tied together by two
flaxen and four papyrus cables, on top of which was laid a
roadway of planks covered by brushwood and earth. These
cables were later brought to Athens as war trophies (Herodotus 9. 121).

72 The sea, which the Greeks invested with varying degrees of
supernatural power, submits to the humiliation of yoking.
This was an act of impiety (see 722–23 and 745–48, with
notes).

73– The stanza "belongs to" XERXES, and the heroic magnifi-
80 cence of his expedition is enhanced by echoes of Homeric
vocabulary; for example, "furious" (thourios) is an epithet
for Ares in The Iliad.

80 The "race born of gold" suggests the myth of Persian descent
from Perseus, begotten on Danae by Zeus in a shower of
gold.
    a godlike man: a Homeric cadence.

A *murderous viper's glance,*
With many men and many ships,
Driving his Syrian car,
He thrusts against men famed for the spear,   85
An Ares who fights with the bow.

ANTISTROPHE 2

No race of men, however renowned,
Can resist such a raging flood,
Can stem with walls built thick and true
An irresistible wave of the sea.   90

---

82   The image is drawn directly from Homer (*The Iliad* 22. 93–95).

84   *Syrian* was the Greek term for "Assyrian" (Herodotus 7. 63). This and the next two lines are modeled closely on a verse in a Delphic oracle, which Herodotus says was delivered to the Athenians in 480: "sharp Ares driving his Syrian-bred car" (7. 140).

85–   The Persian bow is contrasted with the Hellenic spear (see
86   note on 51). The Greek attitude is perhaps best shown by the comment Herodotus gives to Aristagoras the Milesian, who tried to enlist Athenian support for the Ionian revolt in 499 B.C. with the argument that "[the Persians] were accustomed to use neither shield nor spear, and would be easy to overcome" (5. 97. 1).
     Ares: a common equivalent of "war."

87–   To speak of a "flood" of men has of course become a poetic
90   commonplace (cf. 412). Here the metaphor can be termed "Homeric" in that we almost lose the point of departure in 89–90 and hear, with its wonderful sonority, of the *wave of the sea,* (*kuma thalassas*).

89   Walls *thick and true* seems to be an intentional echo of *marshals strong and true* in 79.

For the Persian army cannot be withstood,
Their men are mighty of heart.

MESODE

But what mortal can escape
God's crafty snare?
Whose foot is so light   95
That he can leap aside?
Man is coaxed in seeming goodwill

---

91   The metaphorically *irresistible* (*amachon*) *wave* of 90 is explained more literally by the army that "cannot be withstood" (*aprosoistos*).

93–   I have translated these lines in the order in which they
114   appear in the manuscripts, although 93–100 and 101–14 are usually inverted by modern editors. (The poetic logic of the manuscript order is ably defended by W. C. Scott in *Greek, Roman & Byzantine Studies* 9 [1968] 259–66.) I have also retained Murray's designation of 93–100 as a "mesode," in preference to Broadhead's attempt to turn them into a matching pair of stanzas by emendation.

93–   A modern reader finds the theology of these lines difficult to
100   comprehend; that God should be responsible for a man's ruin seems inconceivable. Yet it is typically Greek, and found as early as *The Iliad* 19. 86–87, where Agamemnon says: "I am not responsible [for offending Achilles], but Zeus, and Fate, and Erinys who walks in the dark." The primary application here is to the Greeks: they were deceived, the CHORUS says, into thinking they could withstand the invincible Persians; but we hear another, darker, overtone, by which the Persians and their king will be shown to be the real victims of this divinely-inspired delusion.

94   With *God's crafty snare* (more literally, "deception"), Broadhead aptly compares Aeschylus' fragment 301n.: "God does not shun just deception." Cf. also 724–25 below.

31

To *the net of ruin,*
From which he cannot
Escape unscathed.   100

STROPHE 3

For Fate ordained from God
Long ago decreed,
Enjoined upon the Persians
Destruction of walls, waging of wars,
The furious cavalry charge   105
And cities' fall.

ANTISTROPHE 3

They then learned to watch
The broad path of sea
Grow gray from wind's raging,   110

---

98 *Net of ruin* is Hermann's brilliant emendation, close to
   what the manuscripts offer and thoroughly Aeschylean (cf.
   Prometheus Bound 1078). "Ruin" (*Atē*) and "deception"
   (*apatē*, 94 above, with note) are connected by a false ety-
   mology elsewhere in Greek literature (cf. *The Suppliants*
   110–11).

101 The latent personification of *Moira, Fate* (literally, "Allot-
   ter"), is here given renewed life by the verb, which suggests
   that the Persians were "overmastered" by their destiny to
   conquer.

102 The Greek verb translated *enjoined* likewise implies that
   the command was laid upon them, a burden, as it were,
   whose obligation they must discharge.

104 The English is too pale for the vigorous Aeschylean phrase,
   "wall-splitting wars."

109 "Broad-wayed" or "gray" are favorite Homeric epithets for
   the sea; what is new is Aeschylus' invention of a verb to
   catch the very process by which the wind turns the sea gray.

Trusting the ships whose slender cables
Cunningly contrived to bear
Their burden of men.

STROPHE 4

These are thoughts that rend   115
My black-robed heart with fear.
O for the Persian armament!
May the city not hear this cry,
The great citadel of Susa empty of men.

ANTISTROPHE 4

The Cissian city will sing   120
In antiphonal echoing cry,
O—and a thronging crowd of women

113– The translation attempts to retain the ambiguity of the
114   original: whereas the lines suggest the bridge of boats across
the Hellespont (see 722 and note), there is nothing in them
which is not strictly applicable to a ship's function of trans-
porting men.

115– When the poet writes "my heart [or mind], dressed in a
116   black *chitōn*, is torn with fear," he is doing more than merely
giving his poetic fancy free rein; he is suggesting the Greek
and Asiatic reaction to news of disaster, a rending of garments, a result made explicit at 125. The boldness of the
image results from the fact that it is merely *fear* for the
future that has this effect, while the atmosphere of gloom is
increased by the black robes in which the heart is somewhat
daringly said to be dressed. (For a similar image, see 161.)

120– *Cissian:* see note on 17.

121   *sing:* an emendation, admitted by most editors. (At *The
Libation Bearers* 423–24 we hear of a "Cissian mourning
woman," with which compare 939 and 1054 below, and
notes.) The vivid reality of the aftermath is brought out by

Will take up this mournful shout
And fine linen robes will be torn with grief.   125

STROPHE 5

For all the horse-driving mass of men
And the tramping troops of men on foot,
Like a swarm of bees have gone away
Streaming after the lord of the troops,
Have crossed the bridge that yokes   130
Both necks of land
One to another.

ANTISTROPHE 5

And marriage-beds are filled with tears
Of wives who long for their absent men.

---

use of the future *indicative* tense (where a subjunctive might be expected): the disaster has already occurred; shouts of lamentation resound and garments are rent in grief.

128– It is clearly appropriate to compare the progress of the
129 army behind its leader to a swarm of bees, both in their numbers and in the somewhat irregular, triangular, zigzag pattern such a swarm makes.
    lord of the troops: an unmistakable Homeric echo.

130ff I have necessarily simplified the original.

133– The utter simplicity of this picture adds to its pathos. The
139 contrary themes of the Persian expedition's splendor and size on the one hand and the broadly hinted fear and foreboding on the other have been played against one another in forceful counterpoint. Here the effect caused by the expedition's departure is summarized in a tender portrayal of personal loss. More movingly than the above translation, 133 suggests that it is the very beds which long for their absent men. The Persian women are introduced only in 135 and

The Persian women in delicate grief,　　　　　　135
Each in a longing full of love
For the warrior mate she sent
With fond farewell,
Is left alone.

Come now, O Persians, who are seated here　　　140
At this ancient abode,
Let us ponder in thought, anxious and deep
　　—For the matter is pressing—
How things have turned out for Xerxes the King
Born of Darius,　　　　　　　　　　　　　145

---

are characterized by the fine adjective *habropentheis,* "in
delicate grief" (the Persians' lament "with delicate step,"
habrobatai, at 1072): their grief is a refinement of the
luxury in which they live (see 3, 9, especially 42—*habrodiai-
tōn,* "lovers of luxury"—45, 53, 79–80). *Mate* in 137 is,
more literally, "bedmate" and picks up "beds" in 133,
whereas *With fond farewell* in 138 recalls the scene of leave-
taking.

137　*warrior:* not an adequate equivalent of the Greek phrase,
"furious spear-armed *(mate),"* which reminds us of *anvils
of the spear* at 51 and the *furious lord* of 73.

140–　The lyric section of the entrance song is over, and the
149　CHORUS returns to anapestic rhythm; the lines are probably
delivered by the leader of the CHORUS alone.

141　*ancient abode:* It is impossible to be certain to what this
phrase refers; the royal palace, DARIUS' tomb, or the Elders'
Council Chamber (as in Phrynichus' play) have all been
suggested. (See above, p. 23, stage direction prefixed to play.)

142　*thought:* The Greek word, *phrontis,* often has the connotation of "anxious care," an effect increased by *bathyboulon,*
"ponder(ing) deep." The objection that the CHORUS cannot
ponder about "how XERXES is faring"—they can only hope
to obtain further information—seems unnecessarily literal.

35

Whether Persians have won by drawing their bows
Or the strength of the Greeks'
    Pointed spears has prevailed.

    The QUEEN *enters in a chariot drawn by at-*
    tendants.

But here comes the lady mother of our king   **150**
Whose radiant glance vies with the gods,
    My Queen. I fall down and adore.

147– The text does not say "Persian" *bows* or "Greek" *spears,* but
149   the two weapons are chosen by metonymy as iconographically
      suited to the opposing parties.

149   "Strength of the spear" is a faintly Homeric periphrasis (in
      Homer, generally with a proper name).

150– The QUEEN's later mention of entering "without a chariot"
151   (see 607–8, with note) indicates that her entry here is in a
      chariot and with full retinue. Her arrival is heralded by a
      fittingly elaborate conceit: she is a "light to rival the gaze of
      gods." The radiance of her countenance is here made to
      stand for the splendor of her appearance generally and
      evokes a reverential, almost worshipful response from the
      CHORUS, "her humble servants." This note of devotion is
      caught, too, by the simple cadence, "mother of our king . . .
      My Queen." *Comes* in line 150 does not catch the element
      of haste (and, by implication, urgency) in the Greek.

152   *I fall down* . . . : No Greek audience could respond to this
      word with anything but repugnance. Whether the Asiatic
      of the fifth century B.C. actually thought of his royalty as
      divine is a moot point, perhaps best left to the historians of
      religion to settle; the act of prostration, at any rate, sug-
      gested divine worship, and even in that context would have
      been too physically demeaning to come easily to a Greek,
      as Alexander was to discover. How much more is in this line
      than merely a touch of authentic color? It is difficult to say
      with certainty, but it is at least possible that Aeschylus is

We must all now hail her
  With welcoming words of address.

Lady, first of Persian women, those who wear the flowing
    dress,   155
Reverend lady, Xerxes' mother, hail to you, Darius' wife.
Consort of the God of Persians, mother also of their God,
If their ancient lucky fortune hasn't now abandoned the
    troops.

QUEEN *Listen, now, to why I come from out of the*
       palace's golden halls,

---

using it here to draw a sharp distinction between Persian
mores and Greek, between upright recognition of the divine
order and fawning prostration before the merely regal.

155ff See "Metrical Schema," p. 17.

156 *Reverend:* more literally "aged"; she had been the wife of
Cambyses, who ascended the throne in 529 B.C., but was
young enough to have had four sons by DARIUS after he became king in 522. She seems to have been born about 550
and would therefore have been seventy at the dramatic date
of the play.

157 The deification of the Persian royal house, already implicit
in 150 and 152, is here made quite clear: "of a god of Persians the wife, of a god the mother. . . ."

158 This line introduces, for the first time in the play, the important motif of the "ancient spirit" of divinely sent good
fortune (see "Introduction," pages 14–16) which, inconstant
and potentially dangerous, can leave a man, Greek as well
as Persian, in the lurch. The line is thoroughly Herodotean
in its theology.

159 The manuscripts here identify the speaker as "Atossa," but
the audience would not have had programs, and she is not
identified by name in the dialogue; I therefore follow Wilamowitz and Murray in styling her simply "Queen." Her

From the chamber which we shared, the former king, Darius
and I.   160
Anxious thoughts now tear apart my heart. To you, then, I
shall speak
Fears that grip me, fears from which I see no way to flee, my
friends:
Riches, surging forward in a cloud of dust, may trample down
True prosperity which Darius won with help from one of the
gods.
Double is the care (which I can hardly utter) in my heart: 165

---

first words echo again the splendid wealth of the Persian dynasty, now risked in a far-flung expedition. The possible loss of this wealth, it turns out, is an obsessive fear of the aged Queen.

162– A difficult passage. The Queen's meaning is obscured by the
164 opaque way in which she expresses it. What she appears to say is that she fears that "great wealth, having raised a cloud of dust on the ground, may with its foot [?] overturn prosperity (which Darius won . . .)." There is no difficulty in the concept of "wealth overturning prosperity." It was a commonplace in Greek thought that true prosperity (*eudaimonia*, or as here, *olbos*) was not to be confused with merely material possessions (*ploutos*, lucre); excessive grasping after the latter might even endanger the former. Matters are complicated by the fact that wealth is often mentioned as a constituent part of prosperity, and the two terms are sometimes used synonymously (as in 250, 252, and 755–56).

164 *prosperity: olbos*; cf. 252, 709, 756, 826. The suggestion will be made explicit that Xerxes' intemperate grasping destroyed the Persians' long-accumulated prosperity.

with help . . . gods: more than pious proviso, it hearkens back to the *daimōn*, who is about to transfer his allegiance, and fits into the larger pattern of Xerxes' rashness as part of a divine plan.

165– Again the Queen's thought is veiled in obscurity. The
167 "double care" (165) is specified in the following two lines,

*Wealth when men are gone may not be held in honor by the
     crowd;*
*Men who lose their wealth have not the radiant strength that
     once they had.*
Wealth there is enough, no fear of that; my fear is for the eye,
*Eye of the house, I mean, the master's presence in it, safe and
     sound.*

---

and the first, 166, makes satisfactory sense: she is afraid that
the riches of the royal house, bereft of the men who acquired
and now preserve them, may not be enough to keep the
throngs of subjects in check. Strange as it sounds, the
Queen seems to be expressing fears of revolution. But what
of 167? Is it, as Wilamowitz thought, merely a filler, a round-
ing-off of the contrast, more rhetorical than meaningful? It is
certainly hard to see what contrast the poet wished his
character to make: "Money without men is insecure; men
without money are undervalued." Is she really afraid that
Xerxes may squander all the wealth of Persia on an un-
successful Greek campaign and so be held in less esteem
when he returns? (Even so, I suspect corruption in the last
half of 167, which does not make satisfactory sense as it
stands.) Or are we to see in this speech a fifth-century example of "feminine syntax," the Queen (characteristically)
speaking in obscure and even ungrammatical generalizations?
One somehow prefers a less drastic explanation, perhaps the
loss of one or more lines, as well as deep textual trouble.

165   *which . . . utter:* The Greek manuscript would have had
MERIMNAPHRASTOS, without indicating whether the
correct division was *merimn' aphrastos* (as most scholars
assume), "care too terrible to talk about," or *merimna
phrastos*, "care that must be discussed (to purge it)." I have
accepted the former, for it is no real argument against it that
the Queen does, immediately, go on to tell them of it; but
the latter may have been what Aeschylus intended.

168–   The eye, as the most striking and important part of the hu-
169   man face, came to symbolize a person's essence. The Queen's

Therefore, gentlemen, since matters stand like this, be coun-
selors,   170
Give advice to me, O Persians, wise and trusted for your age;
For I know you are the source of every kind of good advice.

CHORUS   *Be assured of this, my lady, Queen of all this*
land, not twice
Must you bid us give such word or deed as in our power lies.
For you now have called upon us, counselors well disposed to
you.   175

QUEEN   *For many nights now I have had as company*
Persistent dreams, since the time my son, raising his force,

---

statement that her "fear is for the eye" would not have
sounded so cryptic to the first audience as it does to us. Nevertheless, she goes on to explain her slightly riddling expression
in the following line.

171– No attempt has been made to render the rhyming effect
172   given by words with similar endings (in this case *pistōmata /*
bouleumata) concluding successive lines. Whether this is a
conscious device to round off the scene (as it certainly is in
Shakespeare) or mere accident we cannot say, although
rhyme generally plays no part in the techniques of ancient
Greek versification.

   trusted: recalls the CHORUS' reference to itself in 3 and
anticipates DARIUS' address in 681.

173– The CHORUS' extremely deferential attitude is apparent in
175   these three lines, which are an elaborate equivalent of "at
your service."

176– For the change in metre, see the "Metrical Schema" in the
214   Introduction. The first twenty-five lines of the QUEEN's
speech are a remarkably vivid and (surprisingly, for one whose
opening lines were so obscure) completely lucid account of
her symbolic dream, the first occurrence in Western dramatic
literature—Homer had anticipated it—of a device which,
to go no farther, reached elaborate proportions in Euripides

Went off to the land of Greece, his purpose to destroy it.
But never did the vision come as clearly as
It did the night just past; I'll tell you about it now: 180
Two women appeared before my eyes, both finely dressed,
The one was fitted out in robes of Persian weave,
The other in Doric dress, and when they came into view
They both were far more striking than real life in size
And faultless in loveliness, and sisters they seemed to be   185
Of the same stock. The one had had allotted to her
And dwelt in the Ionian land, the other a foreign land.
Between these two there seemed to arise an argument;
A quarrel followed and when my son discovered it,

(cf. Hecuba's hair-raising visions in *Hecuba*). It serves to take the audience outside the present situation, to give it a vantage point from which to focus on the action at hand; at the same time, it heightens the feeling that something uncanny, ominous, is about to happen and gives to the whole a dimension which can properly be called "supernatural."

178   The Greek says "land of the Ionians," but the QUEEN must mean mainland Greece. Why does she use a term which would probably have suggested, even to Aeschylus' audience, the Ionian coast of Asia? This seems to be part of a pattern in the play intended to remind the Athenians of their claim to being ancestors of the Ionians and may also refer, in a very subtle way, to Themistocles' attempt to play upon the larger loyalties of the Ionians at the time of the invasion of 480 (see notes on 42 and 950).

destroy: The Greek infinitive happens to have the same spelling as the proper noun, "Persians"; the pun must be intentional.

181–   The symbolism of the dream seems fairly obvious. The
198   woman in Persian dress stands for XERXES' Persian dominions—she towers erect, but nevertheless submits to the yoke. The other, in Dorian robes (which here stands simply as a handy equivalent of "Greek") will not submit to the yoke. XERXES' attempt to harness her, to add Greece to his do-

41

He tried to check them, calm them. Then under his chariot   190
He hitched the two of them and yoked them underneath
Their necks. The one, for all her towering pride, kept quiet
In the gear and held her mouth submissive in the reins,
But the other struggled and tore apart the harness straps
With her hands, and now she pulls it along with her by force   195
Unchecked by bit or bridle, and snaps the chariot pole.
My son is falling to the ground; his father stands
Nearby, Darius, taking pity on him. But when
He sees him, Xerxes tears his robes around his body.
These are the nightly visions that I now retell.   200

When I awoke and rose and washed my hands at a spring

---

mains, will end disastrously for himself. Father Darius stands
by pitying, but also, we may suppose, disapproving.

185 Is there deeper significance in the fact that they are sisters
of the same race, and again that the one holds the territory
of Greece merely as the result of an allotment? Or may
Aeschylus be suggesting that Greece and Persia were of common stock and should not have fought each other?

187 *foreign land:* The text says "barbarian," which to a Greek
meant simply "non-Greek." Because to us it has a strong
pejorative flavor, I have translated it as "foreign" or "for-
eigner" generally throughout the play.

189 The *quarrel,* (*stasis*), with its connotation of "intestine
strife," seems to confirm the suggested interpretation of 185
above.

191 A symbolic yoke, ancestor of the more metaphorical "yoke of
Necessity" in *Agamemnon* 218.

194– The three verbs, each expressive of violent exertion and resist-
195 ance, should be noted. (Those who wish to know in detail
what parts of the chariot are involved may consult Broadhead's commentary.)

199 Compare 1030 below.

201 The portentous dream required some appropriate action,
e.g., the sacrifice described in the following lines, which
would normally be preceded by an ablution to secure both

Of water flowing fair, with sacrifice in hand
I went and stood at the altar, wishing to make libation
To the gods who avert, to whom these rituals are due.
But there I saw an eagle flying toward the hearth   205
Of Apollo's altar; speechless I stood in fear, my friends.
A moment later I saw a hawk circle about,
Then rush at the eagle with flapping wings and tear his head
With its claws. The eagle did nothing more than cower and
        yield
To the hawk. A dreadful sight this was for me to see,   210
Dreadful for you to hear. For you are well aware
That if my son fare well, he'd be a man admired
Of all; if ill—he owes the city no explanations.
If safe, he's ruler of the land just as he was.

---

physical and ritual purity. The purificatory properties of a spring of "living" water were felt to be especially high (see 613).

204   Does the QUEEN have some particular "gods who avert" in mind? Probably not, although it may be that Apollo is among them, since it is his altar she seems to be approaching when the omen occurs.

205–   The tenor of the following omen seems obvious: the weaker
210   bird quite unnaturally attacking the stronger, and the latter doing nothing to defend itself.

211–   So obvious is the omen, in fact, that even the QUEEN suspects
212   what it portends. Even so, the hypothetical nature of her statement, *if my son fare well* . . . , comes as a surprise. The alternative, that he may fail, she can hardly utter.

213   The QUEEN consoles herself by pointing out that XERXES "owes the city no explanations"; she uses a phrase that more literally means "is not accountable," which has a technical ring: at Athens, the annually elected magistrates *were* accountable to the people and had to undergo an audit after their year of office.

213–   The QUEEN has apparently quieted her own *care* of 165, for
214   there she had expressed fear that loss of wealth might lead to

CHORUS *Mother, we would neither want to frighten you*
        by our response,   215
Nor to encourage you by what we say. Go and supplicate the
        gods;
Ask them, if you saw some evil thing, that they avert the ill;
Further, that they may accomplish every good for you, your
        sons,
City, all your friends. And, second, you must pour libations to
Earth and dead in offering; with gracious heart make this
        request: 220

---

a weakening of political power. Now she seems to feel that mere safety will be enough to ensure XERXES' continued rule. This process of arguing oneself into a new, self-reassuring position seems very true to life.

215 *Mother:* This appellation seems slightly odd to us: the CHORUS is composed of elderly councilors who are appealed to constantly for sage advice. However, the word gives just the right note of sympathetic concern and indicates the almost filial respect they feel toward the QUEEN (see 156).

215ff For the change of metre, see the "Metrical Schema" p. 17.

216– The interlocking word-pattern of the original defies transla-
218 tion. "Supplicate" in 216 is more literally "with supplica-
     tions," *prostropais*, and the latter half of this compound is picked up in the next line by "avert" (*apotropēn*). The theme of fulfillment is here introduced, for in the text the CHORUS says "fulfill [*telein*] an averting"; it is this theme that is echoed in 218, *agath' ektelē*, and again in 225, *telein* (see note on 255). The ambiguity of words with the root *"tel-"* ("fulfillment" but also "ritual," such as the QUEEN is being urged to perform), perhaps accounts for its occurrence three times in nine lines.

219– The first part of the CHORUS' advice has been general, to
223 make apotropaic supplication of the betokened ill; it merely chimes in with her already stated intention (203–4). Its advice now becomes specific: pour libations to the earth and

*That your husband Darius, whom you say you saw in last
     night's dream,
Send up blessings from beneath the earth for you and for
     your son,
Crush and darken underneath the ground the opposite of
     these.
Such advice with kindly and prophetic heart I give to you;
Matters will be everywhere well for you, as far as we can
     judge.*   225

  QUEEN *You, the first interpreter of these dreams, are full
     of good intent,
Both for my son and for the house, pronouncing with author-
     ity. . .*

---

the dead. At 220–21 a third bit of advice seems to be added:
pray that DARIUS send benefits from below the earth and sup-
press their opposite ills. There is nothing here to surprise or
shock an audience already informed that the QUEEN's mate
was a god (157); it is, on the contrary, appropriate that this
efficacious Spirit (whom, as the CHORUS reminds the QUEEN,
she has just seen in a vision) should be reckoned among the
divine powers capable of aiding the house, and by his relationship to it, even eager to do so. The detail is of course
also meant to anticipate the later appearance of DARIUS.

224 *prophetic heart: thymomantis,* "one who prophesies by na-
     tive wit . . . not by divine inspiration . . . or by observa-
     tion of signs" (Broadhead).

225 *will be:* more literally, "will be fulfilled" (*telein*).

226 The first utterance after an ominous occurrence was con-
     sidered particularly auspicious; cf. the opening of Book 20
     of *The Odyssey,* where Zeus' omen to Odysseus is confirmed
     by the maid's words.

227f The QUEEN means that they have spoken with innate author-
     ity as elderly counselors. At the same time, there is a note of
     self-persuasion in her words. *May the end bring . . . good,*

May the end bring full accomplishment of good. We shall
*   discharge*
All that you have urged to the gods and loved ones under-
*   neath the earth*
When we go into the house again—but first I wish to know,   230
Friends, the place on earth where people say that Athens can
*   be found.*

> CHORUS   *Far towards the region where Lord Helios de-*
> *clines and sets.*

> QUEEN   *So far a city, then, my son desired to hunt and*
> *to destroy?*

---

she says in her next line (*ekteloito;* see notes on 216–18 and
225), but the ominous implication is, "only the end can tell."

231   The matter of Athens comes in rather abruptly (cf. 285) but
not altogether unnaturally, certainly not merely for patriotic
reasons, as some commentators have asserted. Athens will
play a major part in XERXES' disaster, and Athens may very
well be looming as part of the QUEEN's foreboding, for all
her good hopes. (See 285 and 824, with notes.)

232   "In the region of the settings of the wanings of Lord Sun,"
i.e., the west, has been taken as an extreme example of
Aeschylean fulsomeness of expression, perhaps rightly.

233   There are two difficulties in this line: how it should be punc-
tuated (the arguments in favor of an interrogation mark seem
slightly stronger), and the appropriateness of "hunt," *thēr-*
asai. Broadhead tentatively suggests a more common verb
meaning "to destroy," *porthēsai,* but its very commonness
should perhaps prevent us from introducing it into the text.
Groenboom's suggestion of a hunting metaphor seems to be
along the right lines. The picture of Athens as a hunted and
cornered prey, which in the end turns on the hunter and
destroys him, is an effective one. The verb "desired," *himeirō,*
used of XERXES' eagerness, suggests an irrational, or at least
uncontrollable, desire for battle (cf. *Agamemnon* 940: "it
is not for a woman to crave [*himeirein*] battle").

46

CHORUS *All of Greece would then become the subject vassal of the King.*

QUEEN *What size of army must they have for their defeat to bring this about?* 235

CHORUS *Large enough to work a multitude of troubles on the Medes.*

QUEEN *What do they possess besides their men? Is there sufficient wealth?*

CHORUS *Silver springs run through their soil, a treasure from the earth for them.*

QUEEN *Does their prowess show itself in archer combat, using bows?*

CHORUS *Not at all. They stand and fight in close array with spear and shield.* 240

---

234 The line of thought here is: "If Athens is so far away, why did XERXES go after it so eagerly? Because if Athens had fallen, all the rest of Greece would have come under his yoke." Obviously, motives of patriotism on the part of an Athenian poet cannot have been entirely absent, but the view is substantially that of Herodotus (7. 139), whose admiration for Athens was not blind or uncritical.

236 I have translated what the context requires, although the Greek must be tortured to yield that meaning, and two verses may have fallen out after 235, as some scholars have thought. Schenkl's "yes (*nai*, in fact written above *kai* in 236), so large an army that . . ." may be correct.

237– I have retained the order of lines in the manuscripts, which
240 is followed by the Oxford text.

As we have already seen, the QUEEN has national wealth and its stability through political vicissitude very much in mind (163, 168); she now turns to the source of the enemy's wealth, and the CHORUS' reply (238) must have suggested to most of the audience the new veins of silver struck at Mar-

QUEEN   *Who is set as shepherd or as lord to oversee the*
host?

CHORUS   *Slaves of no one are they called, nor in subjec-*
tion to any man.

QUEEN   *How then can they stand against the shock of*
enemy assault?

CHORUS   *Well enough to have destroyed Darius' large and*
expert force.

QUEEN   *Fearful are your words to brood upon for parents*
of the men.   245

CHORUS   *Soon, it seems to me, you'll learn a full and ac-*
curate account.
For here a runner comes whose manner is a Persian courier's,
Bringing news of some event which we shall hear, for good or
ill.

---

oneia in southeast Attica (Herodotus 7. 144; *Const. of Athens*
22. 7). Nor can they have failed to remember, as Aeschylus
intended them to, that it was Themistocles who persuaded
the Athenians to use this new-found wealth to build a navy
in 483 B.C. (see further my *Political Background,* 15).

241–   This magnificent exchange, when recited in a modern pro-
242   duction of *The Persians* at Athens in the summer of 1965,
brought the audience to its feet with cheers and applause in
a spontaneous outpouring of patriotism—exactly as it must
have done in 472 B.C.

243   The QUEEN can only understand military success based on
iron discipline—the Spartan system, in fact. The Athenian
response was a self-impelled willingness to fight, even to die,
for their city, grounded in genuine affection for it; Pericles
in Thucydides' *Funeral Speech* could tell his hearers to become lovers of Athens (2. 43).

244   A reference to Marathon; there is a clear inconsistency between this and the claims made by and for DARIUS later (see
781 and 861–64).

A MESSENGER arrives, in haste and obvious
agitation, through the left passageway.

MESSENGER   O cities of the whole extent of Asia's land,
O Persian land and harbor that enfolds great wealth,   250
A single stroke has brought about the ruin of great
Prosperity, the flower of Persia fallen and gone.
Oh oh! To be the first to bring bad news is bad;
But necessity demands the roll of suffering
Be opened, Persians: the whole barbarian troop is lost.   255

STROPHE 1

CHORUS   Dread, O dread disaster terrible,

249– The MESSENGER appears and delivers his horrible tale of
289   death and destruction, made all the more stark by his use of
      iambics, the metre for factual recitations. The CHORUS punc-
      tuates his delivery with emotional outbursts in lyric metres.

250   "Great harbor of wealth" is a striking metaphor, and the
      suggestion is, I think, that just as wealthy cargo comes into
      a port, so by a reverse process, goods of value are shipped out;
      here, the note of emptying, not fully sounded, nevertheless
      resonates ominously in the background.

251   The destruction of XERXES' force at one blow (i.e., at Sala-
      mis) is one of the dominant themes of the play.

252   Once again, prosperity, olbos, and wealth, ploutos (250),
      are closely linked. Wealth may provide the underpinnings,
      but what is destroyed is far less tangible, far more valuable,
      and its loss far more tragic than mere financial disaster.

254   The tale of suffering is unrolled as if it were a papyrus roll.

255   The whole disaster is reported in a telegraphic message of
      five Greek words.

256– As before, only rough equivalence has been attempted be-
289   tween stanzas within a pair which correspond closely in the
      original.

      The MESSENGER's spoken iambic couplets are bound to

Unheard of. O shed tears, Persians,
  As you hear this woe:

MESSENGER *That all that expedition is utterly destroyed;* 260
And I myself did not expect to return alive.

ANTISTROPHE 1

CHORUS *Too long our lives have proved, we are*
Too old to hear of this affliction
    Unexpected.   265

MESSENGER *I did not hear an account from others, I was*
      there,
Persians, and can tell details of the disaster.

---

the CHORUS' sung laments by links both verbal and grammatical, and it is this interweaving of the emotional and the horribly factual that gives this section its peculiar power.

256 The sound of the word translated as "dread" has the same first syllable as the cry in the next line, *aiai*; between these two words the syllable is heard in the middle of *dai* ("terrible") and again in the word which means "shed tears". The effect is of one long, grammatically contained wail.

257 *shed tears:* almost, in the Greek, "drench yourselves."

260 The MESSENGER's couplet picks up the CHORUS' "hear this woe"; "[namely] that . . ." he replies.

261 As men do who have escaped disaster, the MESSENGER adverts for a moment to his own unexpected safe arrival.

263 The CHORUS answers the MESSENGER's implication that he might have died young by retorting that their *own* lives (heavily emphasized by the choice and order of words) have been too long. In 265 they echo the MESSENGER by calling the affliction "unexpected."

266 The MESSENGER in turn picks up the CHORUS' "hear of this affliction" and turns it around: "I didn't hear of it from others; I was [all too dreadfully, as the particles again imply] *there*."

STROPHE 2

CHORUS   *Oh oh oh oh . . . in vain*
The profuse variety of weapons
Went from the Asian land   270
To the enemy land of Greece.

MESSENGER   *The shores of Salamis and all the coast*
                   around
Are full of corpses of men most miserably destroyed.

ANTISTROPHE 2

CHORUS   *Oh oh oh oh . . . dear ones'*
Bodies which you say are borne   275
Sea-drenched and swirling,
Bobbing in their robes.

268– The general gist is clear: the Persians' weapons for all their
271   variety, effected nothing; "in vain" sounds the keynote; but
      the text at 270 seems rather hopelessly redundant. The sym-
      bolism of Oriental bow *versus* Hellenic spear is here aban-
      doned in favor of a single word, "(weapons) all mixed in,"
      which gives a vivid picture of the great profusion and variety
      of the dress and weapons of the various contingents in
      XERXES' army (for the details, see Herodotus 7. 40–41).

272   *Salamis:* pronounce *Sal'-e-miss.*
      In Greek the MESSENGER's first word is "there are filling
      up . . . ," with emphasis on the quantitative size of the
      disaster, which woefully balances the great quantities of men
      in the original expedition.

273   The first word in this line brings before the audience for the
      first, but not the last, time in the play the name of Salamis,
      where (for Aeschylus' purpose, at least) the entire Persian
      defeat has been compressed into one engagement.

275– Once more, the text shows signs of deep corruption; this is
277   particularly unfortunate here, for the exact nuances of some
      of these images are thus beyond recovery. According to the
      revised version, the corpses are "sea-dipped" and "much-

51

MESSENGER No *use to the army were their bows; the
entire force*
Perished, overcome by ram-thrusts from the ships.

STROPHE 3

CHORUS *Send up a wail, a cry*   280
Unlucky, horrible for the wretched
Persians, for all their plans are now
Ruined. Aeee, the army destroyed.

MESSENGER *O name of Salamis, most hated name to
hear!*
Ah, how I lament when I remember Athens.   285

ANTISTROPHE 3

CHORUS *Athens hateful to foes!*

---

swirled," although the manuscripts have "sea-swirled" and
"much-dipped." The exact wording of 277 cannot be restored; a picture of the Persians' great robes eddying in the
currents of the straits suggests itself.

280– In the original, the woeful *ai*-sounds are again heard, three
281 times in two lines.

282– The text degenerates once again (choral utterances, where
283 there is often little factual content to help the scribe along,
being particularly prone to such corruption), so that any
translation is to some extent guesswork.

285 The audience cannot have failed to detect here a reference
to what must have been a very famous story. As Herodotus
tells it (5. 105), after the failure of the first Persian expedition against Greece in 490, DARIUS wore Athens as a hair
shirt: he made his slave repeat to him three times as he sat
down to dinner, "Master, remember the Athenians." The
story is referred to again at 824, and it is possible that
it derives ultimately from Aeschylus.

We, too, have cause to remember,
For they made so many Persian wives
Wives no more, stripped of their men.

> The MESSENGER and CHORUS look to the
> QUEEN, who after an additional period of si-
> lence, at last speaks.

QUEEN   *I have long been silent, wretched, struck outside*
   my wits   290
With horrors; this disaster shocks and overwhelms,
Prevents the speaking of, or asking, what befell.
And yet necessity dictates that men should bear
The ills the gods bestow. So take your stand, unroll
The suffering, even if your tale be told with groans: 295
Who has survived, and which of the leaders of the troops
Shall we lament, the men whose places of command
Were left vacant by their dying, and none to fill them up?

MESSENGER   *Xerxes himself still lives and looks upon the*
   light.

290– The QUEEN has heard the exchanges between the CHORUS
293   and the MESSENGER, has learned the substance of the disaster, and has been brought to *feel* it (with the audience)
on the emotional, because lyrically expressed, level of the
CHORUS. Now, after a long silence, she reacts with stunning
simplicity and force. The impact of 290–93 is increased by
the utter plainness of the diction.

293– A cardinal tenet of Aeschylean faith; compare *The Seven*
294   *Against Thebes* 719 (in very similar, almost "formulaic,"
language): "no one can escape the ills the gods send."

294– The metaphor of the papyrus-roll is here expanded: the her-
295   ald is to take his stand and read it, as it were, a proclamation.

296   The QUEEN's thoughts turn first to the *living*, entirely naturally for a mother who hopes her son may yet be alive.

QUEEN A light, a great one, you have mentioned for my
 house,   300
A bright day dawning after the gloomy dark of night.

MESSENGER But Artembares, leader of ten thousand horse,
Is buffeted along Sileniae's hard coasts.
And the chiliarch, Dadakes, by a spear's assault
Leapt out—alas, too light a leap—down from his ship. 305
Tenagon, truest-born of all the Bactrians,
Ranges about the sea-struck shore of Ajax's isle.
Lilaios, Arsames, with Argestes third

300– To the MESSENGER's news that XERXES yet *looks upon the*
301 *light,* the ordinary Greek equivalent of "lives," the QUEEN
  responds with the strikingly simple images of a great light
  and dawn after darkness; she had said, in a similar vein, that
  the master's presence is a house's eye (169).

302– The MESSENGER now settles down to a factual account, a
330 catalog of war dead among the Persian commanders. The
  speech is noteworthy, too, for the variety of its synonymous
  expressions for Salamis, the scene of the disaster.

303 The ancient commentator informs us that Sileniae was the
  name of that part of the coast of Salamis near "Victory
  Point" (probably the Cynosoura peninsula) which must
  have been given its name from this battle.

304 *chiliarch:* a "commander of a thousand." Broadhead, citing
  Herodotus (7. 81), notes that "the units of the Persian army
  were tens or multiples of ten"; their commanders had corresponding names (chiliarch of a thousand, myriarch of ten
  thousand, etc.).

305 A "light leap" is ironical: Dadakes never jumped down from
  his ship so effortlessly, and never will again.

306 "The Bactrii or Bactriani lived in the basin of the upper
  Oxus; their capital was the modern Balkh" (W. W. How and
  J. Wells, *Commentary on Herodotus* i. [Oxford, 1912] 284).

307 *Ajax's isle:* Salamis; cf. *The Iliad* 2. 557, 7. 199; and Sophocles' *Ajax* 134–35.

Now beat against the island's rugged shore, where doves
Find nurture, the island which conquered them and
    brought them down.   310
Of those who neighbor on the springs of Egypt's Nile,
Pharnouchos fell, along with three from a single ship:
Arkteus, Adeues, joined by Pheresseues third.
From Chrysa, Matallos, commander of ten thousand, died;
His yellow, shaggy, thickly-shadowing beard he wet   315
And changed its color in a purple bath of blood.
And Arabos the Magus, and Bactrian Artabes,

309– The dove-breeding island is again Salamis, according to the
310 ancient commentator, the "Scholiast."

310 My translation is a makeshift, as no suitable suggestion has
been made for the improbable verb in the manuscripts
("being conquered").

311– A string of names like this, where there is little control from
316 the context, is naturally susceptible to scribal error, very often
in the form of disarrangement of lines. The order is that of
Broadhead's text.

314 *Chrysa*: probably the same place as the town near Troy
mentioned in the first book of *The Iliad*. I wonder whether
the poet did not intend here a pun on this Persian's name,
Matallos; with the change of one letter (*Metallos*) it might
mean "Mine, of Gold."

315– Such a two-line description of a personal detail of a fallen
316 warrior is directly reminiscent of Homer, where the possible
tedium of lists of names in battle descriptions is relieved by
sidelights (the cinematic technique of "flashback") on their
backgrounds, parentage, appearance, etc. Here the blood-
bath image looks forward to Agamemnon's murder (*Agamemnon* 1389–92, a more detailed and more horrible picture).

317 I have taken the proper name to be "Arabos," his designation
as a member of the priestly caste of Magians. Alternately,
though with less likelihood, his name may be "Magos," described as "the Arabian."

Leading a troop of thirty thousand dusky horse,
Immigrant to a cruel land, who there was slain.
Amistris and Amphistreus, who wielded a spear   320
Destructive, and noble Ariomardos, whose arrows
Apportioned grief, and Seisames, who came from Mysia;
And Tharybis, the lord of five times fifty ships,
A Lyrnaean by birth, a handsome man as well,
Lies dead, a victim of a none too lucky fate.   325
And Syennesis, surpassing all in bravery,
Commanding the Cilicians, who singly caused
Most trouble to the enemy, died gloriously.
Of such heroic leaders I have made report,
Relaying a selection from a stock of ills.   330

QUEEN   O grief! I hear this summit of disasters now,
Disgrace to Persians and calling forth our shrill laments.
But tell me this, turn back to your account again:
The multitude of ships the Greeks had, was it so great

---

319   *Immigrant*: a semitechnical word (and so a metaphor here),
      meaning a noncitizen who has the right of residence and
      certain other judicial rights (cf. the technical term, "landed
      immigrant").

321   "Arrow-points" is Broadhead's all-but-certain emendation.

324   "Lyrna" should probably be identified with Lyrnessus in the
      Troad, mentioned in *The Iliad* (according to the ancient
      geographer, Stephanus of Byzantium).

325   The simplicity of the diction and the understatement (tech-
      nically, "litotes") combine to give a pathetic touch.

326– "When the Cilicians accepted Persian vassalage they were
327   permitted to retain their native kings, who regularly bore the
      name Syennesis" (Broadhead, citing A. T. Olmstead, *History
      of the Persian Empire* [Chicago, 1948] 39).

332   The Greek says, more vividly, that the MESSENGER's reports
      are "disgraces . . . and lamentations."

333– The QUEEN, supposing, naturally enough, that only superior-
336   ity of numbers could account for a Greek victory, turns back

They thought they could join battle with the Persian force, 335
Relying solely on the ram-thrusts of their ships?

MESSENGER   Be sure of this, that in a matter of sheer numbers,
The ships on our side would have conquered, for the Greeks'
Entire total of ships was only three hundred ten,
And of this number ten were specially reserved.   340
But the multitude of ships in Xerxes' fleet—I know
The facts—were no less than a thousand, those in speed
Surpassing, two hundred seven. This is the total sum.
Was it here you think we were surpassed when battle came?
No, not by numbers, but some Spirit crushed the host,   345
Threw in an evil fate against us in the scales.
The gods are keeping the Goddess Pallas' city safe.

---

to the MESSENGER's words at 278–79, where he had referred to "ram-thrusts from the ships."

339–
340

How many ships? The Greek will bear either the interpretation, "300 ships in all; of these, 10 were specially chosen," or "the whole [main] contingent numbered 300, but apart from these, 10 . . ."; that is, a total of 310. It is possible that in giving the number 300 in the form "ten thirties" in the original Greek of 339, the MESSENGER may be referring to an actual manner of numbering the Greek fleet.

341–
343

This total of 1,207 for the Persian fleet was to become sacrosanct (cf. Herodotus 7. 89, 184), and all later figures, e.g., in Isocrates and Diodorus, may derive from Aeschylus.

345–
346

"Not by numbers," the MESSENGER says, "but by some daimōn" ("Spirit" is the best English can do; "divine power" would be closer). The word stands for any (undifferentiated) force or agency, on the more than human level, without the personal overtones of theos or theoi (god, gods). For a discussion of the daimōn-theme, see "Introduction," pages 14–16.

Whereas the meaning of the image in 346 is clear, its details are not quite distinct. I take it to mean that the daimōn "unbalanced the scales by throwing in an unequal [i.e., heavier] weight of [evil] fortune [against us]."

QUEEN   What? The city of Athens still remains intact?

MESSENGER   As long as there are men, there is a staunch
defense.

QUEEN   But tell us of the first encounter by the ships: 350
Which ones first began the battle, whether Greeks,
Or my son, in proud reliance on his throng of ships?

MESSENGER   The one that started the whole disaster,
   lady, was
Some Curse or Evil Spirit which appeared from somewhere.
For a man, a Greek, arrived from the Athenian camp   355

---

347   The line is beautifully balanced in Greek: "gods the city
save of Pallas [Athena] the goddess." The Greeks had stood,
as an anonymous contemporary writer put it, "on the razor's
edge": it was only the gods that kept them from falling the
wrong way.

349   When, in the councils before the battle of Salamis, Adei-
mantus, the Corinthian general, tried to silence Themistocles
on the grounds that the enemy already held Athens and so
he had no city to speak for, Themistocles retorted, "We have
a city greater than yours, as long as we have two hundred
ships full of men" (Herodotus 8. 61). The Scholiast quotes
a line from Alcaeus, the early sixth-century poet of Lesbos:
"Men are a city's warlike defense" (fragment 35. 10, Diehl).
Thucydides has the general Nicias say to his men in Sicily,
"Men and not walls make a city" (7. 77. 4), which is itself
reminiscent of Pericles' words in Thucydides (1. 143. 5).
The theme also appears in Sophocles, Oedipus the King
56–57.

354   For the daimōn-theme, see "Introduction," pages 14–16.

355   Herodotus' account (8. 75) makes it clear that Themistocles
sent his foreign slave Sicinnus to the Persian fleet with his
deceptive message. The elimination of this intermediary in
Aeschylus' version, which speaks of "a Greek," has the effect
of throwing Themistocles' agency into heightened relief.

And spoke to your son Xerxes words to this effect,
That once the darkness and the black of night should come,
The Greeks would not remain, but to their rowers' seats
Would leap in disarray, each man for himself,
And run away in secret flight to save their lives. 360
Your son, the moment that he heard, not comprehending
The treachery of the Greek, the jealousy of the gods,
Proclaimed to all his captains the following command,
That when the rays of the sun should cease to scorch the
   earth,
And darkness covered over all the vault of sky, 365
They should order the main body of ships in three divisions

---

356 Again, Herodotus' account differs slightly: there, Sicinnus
delivers the message to XERXES' commanders, who relay the
information. In a matter of such importance it is at least
possible that the admirals, even if approached first, would
have insisted that the man speak to the king directly, but
again, Aeschylus may simply be eliminating a stage in the
process.

357– The straightforward simplicity of the message should be
360 noted, for in later authors from Herodotus on, the content
is fantastically (and unnecessarily) embellished to include
disaffection among the Greek forces, an offer by the Athenians to defect to XERXES, and other such implausible additions.

361 XERXES' reaction is immediate and, by implication, impul-
sive. His failure was a failure of intelligence: he could not
fathom Themistocles' deceitfulness or the gods' jealousy; the
latter backs up and confirms the former, but it is important
to notice which comes first.

366– The *main body* in 366 is clearly to be distinguished from
368 the *others* in 368. The three *divisions* in 366 are probably three columns, as elsewhere in military contexts. The
description is imprecise enough to have generated several
theories about tactics.

To guard the exit routes and straits of sounding sea,
While others were to circle round to Ajax's isle;
That if the Greeks avoided an evil fate of death
By finding some escape in secret with their ships,   370
The order was posted for all his captains, "off with their
    heads."
So many were his words, and from a cheerful heart:
He did not know what was about to come from the gods.
His men, without disorder, but with obedient hearts,
Got them their suppers and each sailor in the crews   375
Attached his oar around its neatly fitted peg.
But when the radiance of the sun had disappeared
And night came on, each sailor, master of an oar,
Went aboard his ship, and all who managed heavy arms.
And line of ships of war called out to other line;   380

---

368   *Ajax's isle:* Salamis. What exactly Aeschylus had in mind
here cannot be determined with certainty. XERXES' objective
of blocking the escape route would be served by stationing a
few ships off the southwestern tip of the island, which is
what this line may be referring to.

371   *off with their heads:* The summary threat fits well the picture
of the oriental despot.

373   Again a failure of XERXES' intelligence.

374   The Persians' good order here is balanced nicely by the
Greeks' orderly attack later (399–400), which is in marked
contrast to what the Greek message had suggested (359).

376   "He fastened his oar [by tying it] to the peg, which was well-
fitted to the oar." The minute detail, minutely described,
is intended to show the calm, unruffled nature of the Persians' preparations.

378–   To distinguish a sailor and marine as *master of an oar* and
379   "overseer" of *heavy arms* respectively may seem extravagant
to us, but is not beyond the possible limits of Aeschylean
diction.

380   It is not clear what the "lines" are. They may be the various
squadrons, with "ships of war" taken collectively; less prob-

The captains kept at oar as each had been assigned.
And all night long the masters of the ships maintained
The sailing back and forth by all the naval host.
And night departed, and the army of the Greeks did not
In any way attempt to sail out in secret.   385
But when the white-horsed chariot of dawn appeared
And filled the entire earth with radiance to behold,
The first thing was a sound, a shouting from the Greeks,
A joyful song, and to it, making shrill response,
From the island rocks about there came an antiphony   390
Of echoes; fear stood next to each one of our men,
Tripped up in their hopes: for not as if in flight
Were the Greeks raising then a solemn paean-strain,
But rushing into battle with daring confidence;
A trumpet, too, blazed over everything its sound.   395
At once, with measured stroke of surging, sea-dipped oar,
They struck the brine and made it roar from one command,
And quickly all of them were visible to sight.
Their right wing first, in order just as they had been
Arranged, led off, and next the whole remaining force   400
Came out to the attack, and with the sight we heard

---

ably, the reference is to the *three divisions* mentioned in
366.

384– The stages are marked effectively for building up suspense:
398   first the "gray" dawn—and no sign of a secret attempt by
      the Greeks to escape. Then (368 ff.) the full blaze of dawn,
      with a Greek response: first a sound, undifferentiated (388),
      then distinguishable as a *song* of triumphant attack (389),
      setting up a veritable litany with the surrounding rocky
      shores. Next the trumpet call is heard (395—a rather strik-
      ing example of *synaesthesia*: a blazing sound), then the
      splash of oars; finally, with abrupt and climactic simplicity,
      "all the men came clearly into sight" (398).

399– It should be remembered that Aeschylus is composing as an
400   eyewitness. The details he gives, therefore, have a greater
      claim to credibility than later accounts.

A loud voice of command: "O sons of Greeks, go on,
Bring freedom to your fatherland, bring freedom to
Your children, wives, and seats of your ancestral gods,
And your forbears' graves; now the struggle is for all."   405
Of course, on our side, too, a roar of Persian tongues
Went forth in answer; the moment would not brook delay.
Immediately ship struck its brazen-plated beak
On ship. The ramming was begun by a Greek ship
And it snapped off from one of the Phoenicians the whole   410
Curving stern, and men on both sides shot their spears.
At first the streaming Persian force withstood the shocks;
But when their crowd of ships was gathered in the straits,
And no assistance could be given one to another,
But they were being struck by their own brazen rams,   415
They kept on breaking all their equipage of oars,
And the ships of the Greeks, with perfect plan and order,
    came

402–   These words only make sense in their context if they were
405   spoken once. i.e., by the commander-in-chief, Themistocles.
       In my opinion there is a good chance that they are an
       iambic rendering of Themistocles' words on this occasion, or
       something very like them.

409   According to Herodotus (8. 84) the first Greek ship to strike
       an enemy was that of Ameinias of Pallene (possibly to be
       identified with Aeschylus' brother of the same name).

412   The choice of words here, a *stream* of the Persian force,
       would seem to indicate that the Persians had by this time
       come deeply into the narrow straits, had, in fact, allowed
       themselves to be lured physically into the trap set by
       Themistocles.

415   With this description should be compared that of the
       storm's effect on the Greek fleet returning from Troy at
       Agamemnon 654ff.

417   Again, as at 399–400, the timing and good order of the
       Greeks are emphasized.

Around them in a circle and struck, and hulls of ships
Were overturned; and the sea no longer was visible,
Filled as it was with shipwrecks and the slaughter of men.   420
The beaches, too, and the reefs around were filled with
    corpses.
Now every ship that came with the Persian armament
Was being rowed for quick escape, no order left.
And they kept striking us, deboning us, like tunnies
Or a catch of fish, with broken fragments of oars, or bits   425
Of flotsam from the wrecks; and all this time, moaning
And wailing held control of that area of sea,
Until the eye of black night took it away.
So great a crowd of ills, not even if I took
Ten days in order to tell, could I tell the tale in full.   430
For be assured of this, that never in one day
Did such a huge number of men go to their deaths.

    QUEEN   Aeee! A huge sea of ills has broken out
And overwhelmed the Persians and all the barbarian race.

    MESSENGER   Be sure of this, you have not yet heard half
    the evil: 435
For such a load of sufferings came after these
That they were twice outbalanced in the scales and more.

---

419   Compare the splendid metaphor at *Agam.* 659, "the Aegean
     sea blossoming with corpses."

422   In Herodotus' account, the advance Persian ships retreated
     in confusion and fell foul of their own rear lines, who were
     still advancing (8. 89).

427   The metaphor is of the sea held captive by wails and lamen-
     tation as by an occupying army.

433   The image has become dull to us through overuse; most
     familiar, perhaps, is Hamlet's "or take arms against a sea of
     troubles." (See also 599–600 and, in similar vein, 90.)

435– The expression is slightly illogical: "The evil is not yet at
437   its half; what follows will twice outweigh it" implies that

QUEEN *What luck could there have been yet more*
adverse than this?
Tell us what misfortune this was you say came on
The troops and swung the balance of disaster down. 440

MESSENGER *Those Persians at their peak of physical*
condition,
Stoutest of heart and of outstanding lineage,
And always in the first the Lord himself could trust,
Were slain disgracefully, a most inglorious death.

QUEEN *Oh I am wretched for this evil chance, my*
friends. 445
What is the death you say that these men met, and
perished?

MESSENGER *There is an island just in front of Salamis,*

---

what had been told is only a *third;* but clearly Aeschylus
means no more than that a greater evil is yet to come.

440 The QUEEN picks up the "scales" motif (see 708).

443 *trust:* The phrase suggests that they might have composed
the king's bodyguard.

444 "A shameful and inglorious incident," Broadhead well remarks, "the seriousness of which was not to be measured by
mere numbers." He aptly compares the effect of the capture
of the nobly born Spartans on Sphacteria Island during the
Peloponnesian War (Thucydides 4. 15).

447 There are two modern contenders for the claim of being
this island (styled Psyttaleia in ancient authorities), Lipso-
koutáli, as most historians believe (an identification which
may go back to the fourth century B.C.; see E. Bayer in *His-
toria* 18 [1969] 640), or St. George (Beloch, Hammond,
Broadhead). As any decision will rest ultimately, in part at
least, on one's reconstruction of the battle, the argument
very quickly risks circularity. Even granting a rise in water-
level, St. George seems too small and too far into the chan-
nel to have been able to play the role that the ancient
authorities assign to Psyttaleia.

A small one, no fit anchorage for ships, where Pan
Who loves the dance, roams along the shore of the sea.
There he had sent these men, so that, if the enemy   450
Took refuge on the island from their ruined ships,
The surviving Greeks would make easy victims for the kill;
Their friends they were to save from shipwreck in the sea—
So false their knowledge of the outcome: for when God
Gave glory in the naval battle to the Greeks,   455
They girt their bodies round with well-made arms of bronze
And leapt from their ships, just as they were, and circled in

---

448– The introduction of an official cult of Pan at Athens was a
449   recent occurrence (Herodotus 6. 105), although as a tradi-
      tional forest and mountain spirit, his name must long have
      been associated with Psyttaleia. Pausanias remarks that
      "wooden [i.e., rude and primitive] images of him could be
      found on the island" (1. 36. 2).

450– Aeschylus is in substantial agreement with Herodotus about
453   the purpose of this maneuver: "The Persians were disem-
      barked on the island so that, when the naval battle took
      place, and men and wreckage would be most likely to be
      washed up there (for the island lay right in the path of the
      impending battle), they might save some and slay others"
      (8. 76).

454– for when God . . . Greeks: This might be merely a manner
455   of speaking—"everyday" piety (e.g., "God forbid")—but the
      phrase gains significance from its place in the pattern of
      divine, or daimonic, causation (see "Introduction," pp. 14–
      16).
      Gave glory: a Homeric phrase.

457   just as they were: The Greek words mean literally "on the
      very day," but I take this to be an example of a compound
      adjective whose first half is the operative one. The whole
      account here gives the impression of an on-the-spot reaction,
      unplanned and somewhat haphazard; Herodotus' version, in
      contrast, has Aristides take "many of the hoplites (heavy
      armed) who were ranged along the shore of Salamis, Atheni-
      ans, across to the island" (8. 95).

From all around the island; the Persians were caught off
  guard
And at a loss for where to turn. They were pummelled by
  rocks
The Greeks threw in profusion, and arrows shot from bow-
  strings   460
Showered down upon the Persians and destroyed them.
At last the Greeks surged forward in a single gush
And struck, and hacked apart their wretched victims' limbs
Until they succeeded in draining out the life from all.
When Xerxes saw the depth of the disaster he shrieked—   465
For he had a seat in full view of the entire army
Atop a lofty hill that neighbored on the sea—

---

458 Who was caught off gaurd, "at a loss," as the Greek has it?
     Certainly the Persians, although the change of subject is not
     signified in the Greek.

465 What XERXES sees is, of course, the whole tide of battle go-
     ing against his men, not the incident on the island.

465– The passage has been condemned, on inadequate grounds,
471   as an interpolation.

466– The location of XERXES' vantage point was disputed: Herod-
467   otus says it was "beneath" Mt. Aegaleos, although in another
      source it was as far away as the border of the Megarian terri-
      tory. XERXES sat on a golden *diphros* (not so much a
      "throne," according to the artistic evidence, as a chair or
      stool) with silver feet, which was long preserved as a relic
      on the Acropolis. Cf. Byron's lines,

> A king sate on the rocky brow
>   Which looks o'er sea-born Salamis;
> And ships, by thousands, lay below,
>   And men in nations;—all were his!
> He counted them at break of day—
> And when the sun set where were they?
>   (*Don Juan* III. lxxxvi. 4)

And tore his robes and let out a shrill and piercing cry;
Immediately passing his orders to the troops on land
He rushed away in disordered flight. To the former one   470
Add this disaster as a subject for laments.

QUEEN   O hateful Spirit! Deceitfully it seems you've
    worked
Upon the Persians' minds. Bitter was the vengeance
My son exacted from famous Athens, and the men
Whom Marathon destroyed before were not enough;   475

---

468   The king's actual tearing of his robes alludes back to the
QUEEN MOTHER's dream (199) and is recalled by XERXES
himself at 1030. XERXES' cries of despair at Salamis (465,
468; the detail seems to be uniquely Aeschylean) will be repeated in the lyric *thrēnos* at the end of the play.

469– Herodotus states that XERXES merely "planned flight" after
470   the battle (8. 97) but waited "for a few days" before actually
withdrawing to Boeotia (8. 113). A disorderly retreat is
emphasized here and in 481, an echo of the Persian ships'
disordered flight from the Salamis straits (422), and in contrast to the Greeks' orderly attack (399–400).

472   The idea seems to be that the *daimōn* "robbed them of
their good sense," although the Greek phrase might also
mean that he "frustrated their intentions." In joining the
notions of "Spirit" and "lies," Aeschylus reminds his hearers
of the opening of the MESSENGER's account of the battle,
where the spiritual agency and the false message of Themistocles are virtually identified (353–55).

473   *Bitter*: that is, the results were unexpected (cf. *Agamemnon*
745, Helen's "bitter marriage-rites" with Paris).

474   *famous*: a standard epithet for Athens: cf. Euripides,
Troades 207, *Hippolytus* 423, 760, 1459, etc.

475   Cf. 244, the only other reference in the play to the Persian
defeat at Marathon (490 B.C.). The contrast between
XERXES' failure and DARIUS' success (864–903) requires that
Marathon be underplayed.

67

For them my son, supposing that he could secure
Requital, drew upon us so great a load of woe.
But you, now, tell us, the ships which escaped destruction,
    where
Did you leave them? Do you know, and can you clearly
    tell?

    MESSENGER   The remaining ships' commanders raised their
      sails in haste   480
And fled in disarray wherever the wind might lead.
The army that was left slowly began to perish
In Boeotian territory, laboring with thirst
For radiant springs, or panting, breathless and ex-
    hausted.
We managed to get across into the Phocians' land,   485
And Dorian country and the gulf of Malia,
Whose plain Spercheios waters with his friendly stream.
From there the land and country of Achaea and
The towns of Thessaly received us, empty as

---

477   The image may be of a fisherman drawing in a catch.

482   The picked force of 300,000, which Herodotus says was left
      behind with XERXES' general Mardonius (8. 113), is here
      ignored (but cf. 796–97).

483– With the manuscript reading, the picture seems to be of the
484   army expiring from thirst, even though within range of the
      "radiance" of spring water (a fine Aeschylean phrase); that
      is, they were too exhausted to make the last few steps to a
      spring. I have, however, preferred a somewhat tamer inter-
      pretation based on an emendation.

485– "The districts through which the retreating army passed are
495   mentioned in their due order" (Broadhead); cf. similar geo-
      graphic descriptions in Aeschylus (*Prometheus Bound* 709–
      35, 829–43; *Agamemnon* 281–311).

487   This is more than geographical trimming; it contrasts pa-
      thetically with the army's terrible thirst a few lines above
      and again in 491.

We were of food. And there it was that most men died   490
Of thirst and hunger; for both of these were present there.
We came into Magnesian country and the land
Of the Macedonians, to the stream of Axios
And Bolbe's reedy marsh, and Pangaeus mountain range,
The land of the Edoni. During the night God raised   495
A storm unseasonably and froze the entire course
Of sacred Strymon's flow; whoever hadn't yet
Believed in gods till then, now prayed and offered vows,
Falling upon his face before the earth and sky.

---

491   Hunger and thirst are portrayed as unwanted attendants upon the retreating army's march. Herodotus' picture of the army's sufferings is equally moving: "Wherever they came to in their march and among whatever peoples, they snatched at and fed upon their crops. If they found no crop, they tore at the grass growing up out of the earth, stripped the bark from the trees, both cultivated and wild, and plucked their leaves and ate that; nothing was left. This they did out of hunger. But plague also, and dysentery, took hold of the army on its march and devastated it" (8. 115).

494– The places are not mentioned in strict geographical order.
495   Mount Pangaeus should come last, after Lake Bolbe, the Strymon River, and the Edoni. There are similar difficulties in some of the geographical data in *Prometheus Bound*, especially the location of certain tribes (the Scythians 709, Chalybes 715, and Amazons 723).

495– The crossing of the Strymon would have taken place no
497   later than early November, and the river would not have been frozen under ordinary circumstances. Either the river froze over (as H. J. Rose believes), or it didn't. If it did, this could be called an "act of God." If it didn't, all we can say is that Aeschylus invented the story to heighten the horrors of the retreat.

497– A realistic touch, one that fits such a "plain man's" narra-
499   tive.

But when the army stopped its repeated invocations,   500
It began to go across the way of solid ice.
And whoever of us hastened across before the rays
Of God's sun were spread managed to get to safety;
For blazing with his rays the bright orb of the sun
Pierced through the path and burned it with his flame: 505
They fell upon each other, and lucky was the man
Whose breath of life was quickest to break out of him.
As many as were left and got through to safety,
After barely managing to struggle across through Thrace,
Have come and made good our escape, not many of us,   510
To our land and hearths. So the Persians' city can lament
In longing for the land's own dearest youthfulness.
These things are true; but I have left out of my account
Many of the ills that God hurled at the Persians.

CHORUS   O Spirit of Suffering, with what a heavy leap—   515
Too heavy!—you jumped upon the entire Persian race.

QUEEN   Ah! I am miserable, the army all destroyed.
O vision that came by night in dreams that were so clear,
Too clearly did you bring your warning of disaster!

---

505   The image seems to be of rays "boring through" the ice.
      Another possible explanation is G. Italie's: "when the sun
      reached the mid-point of its path."

511–   The language is chosen for the pathos it evokes. The *Per-*
512   *sians' city* in 511 is Susa.

512   *the land's . . . youthfulness:* The genitive can be considered
       possessive in two senses: the youth *belong to* the land since
       it raised them (62); but also it has lost its youth and grown
       old, in which sense the phrase is reminiscent of Pericles'
       "the spring has gone out of the year."

517–   The QUEEN reacts to news of the disaster in a thoroughly
531   regal way. Although her words indicate her realization that
       it is "all over" for the Persian force (the army is "finished,"
       517; "this is the way things stand," 525, 527), although she

But you, O men, too lightly judged the evil portent.   520
But still, since this was what your words to me proclaimed,
I wish to make my prayers, first of all to the gods,
Then to earth and the dead I shall take offerings
And come with a libation from within my halls;
—Not for the past; I know that that is over, done—   525
But for the future, if some better thing may come.
So you must now begin from what has happened as fact
And bring to bear on it your counsels in which we trust;
My son, if he should come here before I return,
Address in words of comfort, escort him to the house,   530
To prevent his adding to his store some further harm.

    The QUEEN departs.

CHORUS   O Zeus, who are King, the army of Persians

---

now knows that her visions were correct and the CHORUS'
interpretation of them too blandly optimistic (225), some
pieces of the wreckage must be saved, if only by retaining
her dignity and composure. She will pray to the gods, then
the darker powers, Earth and the dead; the CHORUS is to
take practical counsel, for that, after all, is their role, to be
trusty counselors (2, 142, 171). She closes with thoughts of
her son: they are to console and escort him, and so prevent
the total disaster that any injury to him would constitute.
(Does she think that he may attempt suicide? Wilamowitz
thought her fears were of revolution [cf. 584–90]; but her
words are entirely unspecific, and purposely so; her son must
be preserved from threats the more frightening for being
nameless.)

528   *trust:* cf. 2 and 681.

532–   The women mourn, each for her own man, as the land
597   mourns for all; XERXES (so unlike his father) and the Greek
ships were responsible; Salamis' shores are covered with
corpses mangled by sea and fish. In the last pair of stanzas
the CHORUS turns to the *political* aspect of the disaster: the

With its proud display and its masses of men
You have now destroyed.
The city of Susa, Ecbatana as well   535
*   You have buried in gloomy grief.*
And the veils of many with tender hands
Are torn through,

Persian Empire will crumble now that the absolute power of the king is gone, and freedom (particularly of speech, a Greek preoccupation) will set in. (For the metre, see "Metrical Schema," p. 17.)

532   The destruction of the army is directly attributed to Zeus: a strong statement of one-half of the divine-human "cooperation" by which Aeschylus seeks to explain the Persians' tragedy. It is just possible that Zeus' epithet, "King," is chosen to contrast with what a Greek would have felt to be the illegal despotism of the Persian monarch.

533   In the Greek, a balanced pair of compound adjectives (*megalauchōn* and *poluandrōn*) sums up the main characteristics of the expedition: proud, almost arrogant, hopes of success, and vast numbers of men.

535   The two main cities of the Persian Empire are again paired (see 16).

536   Zeus was originally a sky-god. Here he covers the Persian cities with, as it were, a mist of grief.

537–   The expression of female grief, both as reported and as
545   portrayed on the stage, was to become one of the standard themes of Greek tragedy, as it had been in epic (cf. the laments for Patroclus in Book XIX and for Hector in Book XXIV of *The Iliad*). The details of the description here are chosen to emphasize the delicate luxury of an oriental court, even in its lamentations: *tender hands* (537), *delicate sobs* (541), *with delicate covers* (543), *luxurious pleasure of youth* (544). At the same time, there is excess: veils are gashed (538; cf. the prediction at 125), their bosoms *drenched* with tears (539), their wails most *insatiable* (545). The content is much like that of the fifth antistrophe of the parodos, 133–39.

Their breasts drenched with tears
    As they share in pain.   540
With delicate sobs the women of Persia
Are longing to see their newly wed men;
The beds of their marriage, with delicate covers,
The luxurious pleasure of youth they have lost,
And they grieve with long, insatiable sobs.   545
And I myself, for the death of those gone,
    Shed tears of genuine grief.

STROPHE 1

Now all Asia's land
Moans in emptiness.
Xerxes led forth, oh oh!   550
Xerxes destroyed, woe woe!
Xerxes' plans have all miscarried
In ships of the sea.
Why did Darius then

---

546   *gone:* echoes 1.

547   The exact meaning, and possibly the text, elude us, but Aeschylus seems to have intended that the old men of the CHORUS bear their share of the heavy burden of grief to match the women's share of suffering (540).

548–   The opening lines of this first stanza echo almost exactly 61–
549   62 of the parodos. The vast land of Asia now empty of men makes a striking picture.

550–   The elaborate balance with repetition is hard to achieve in
553   English (there is something to be said for simply transliterating the numerous and varied Greek expressions of grief, *popoi, aiai,* and so forth). The verb that describes Zeus' "destruction" at line 534 is here applied to XERXES.

553   Aeschylus uses an exotic word for "boat," *baris,* for which no convenient equivalent exists in English.

554–   The contrast with DARIUS' success and benevolence (cf. "be-
557   loved" in 557) will become an important theme in the play.

Bring no harm to his men   555
When he led them into battle,
That beloved leader of men from Susa?

ANTISTROPHE 1

Marines and sailors alike
The dark-cheeked, winging
Ships led forth, oh oh!   560
Ships destroyed, woe woe!
Ships with murderous thrusts of their rams
In Ionian hands.
Close was the Lord's escape,
As we hear, when he fled   565
Through the broadly stretching
Blustery ways of Thrace.

STROPHE 2

The first were they to die—oh! oh!
Caught in necessity's grasp—oh!
On the shores of Cychreus' isle—ah!   570

Aeschylus ignores DARIUS' defeats in Scythia and at Marathon to construct an idealised portrait (cf. 652–56).

559 "Wings" is a common metaphor in ancient poetry. For *dark-cheeked*, cf. Homeric "ochre-cheeked."

561 There seems to be a shift from the Persian allies' ships, which "led forth" the Persian troops, to the Greek ships, which rammed and destroyed them.

563 I translate the manuscript reading, rather than a commonly accepted emendation which would make *hands* an additional subject of the verb *destroyed* in 561.

565 Does the CHORUS imply some reservation, some doubt, about the king's safety?

567 *Thrace:* (cf. 509) proverbially "blustery" to the Mediterranean Greeks; cf. 496ff.

570 *Cychreus* (or Cenchreus), an early mythical hero-king of Salamis, is said by Pausanias (1. 36. 1) to have appeared to the Greeks during the battle in the form of a snake.

Are smashed. Moan and snarl,
Shout to heaven your sorrows
In deep lament, ah!
Stretch your pitiful voice
In an agonized howl.   575

ANTISTROPHE 2

Terribly are they torn by the sea—oh! oh!
Mangled by the voiceless children—oh!
Of the unpolluted deep—ah!
Each house grieves for the man
It lost, and childless parents   580
Lament the sorrows, ah!
God sent them in their old age
And hear grief's tale.

STROPHE 3

Those throughout Asia's land are ruled
No longer by Persian laws.   585

571ff The verb in the manuscript has disappeared; *smashed* is
a guess. The imagery in the following lines becomes ferocious
and bestial; their grief has turned them into snarling, howl-
ing animals.

576– The imagery becomes more savage: The bodies are torn by
578 the sea, like wool on a metal comb or criminals on a rack,
and mangled by fish (*voiceless children . . . Of the unpolluted* seems an extravagant periphrasis).

579ff The widows' mourning has been described in 537ff.; now, in
a bold personification, the CHORUS turns to the mourning
of the dead men's homes and aged parents.

582 In the Greek their woes are *daimōni(a)*, supernaturally sent.

584– From the personal and domestic loss the CHORUS turns to
587 the national aspects of the disaster, with its political conse-
quences: the center of authority has lost its grip (note the
vivid present tenses—the disaster has hardly been reported,
but the empire is already crumbling).

75

They carry their tribute no longer,
By a master's necessity fixed,
Nor prostrate themselves to the ground
And adore: for the royal
Strength is destroyed.   590

ANTISTROPHE 3

The tongues of men are no longer kept
In check; for the mass of men
Went loose and free in their speech
When the yoke of strength was loosened.
The fields in Ajax's isle,   595
Awash with blood, hold
Persia's remains.

The QUEEN reappears, on foot this time and
with offerings for the dead.

QUEEN My friends, whoever has experience of troubles,
knows

---

586 The size of the tribute which the Persian king received impressed the Greeks; cf. Herodotus 3. 92.

588–
590 As the crowning insult, obeisance will no longer be made to the king's supremacy.

591–
594 I think it is possible to detect faint traces of a Greek viewpoint in the CHORUS' fear that loosening the yoke of royal strength will mean an end to repressive silence and an increase in (typically democratic) freedom of speech. In *Prometheus Bound* the CHORUS warns Prometheus that he is "too free in his speech" for the tyrant Zeus' liking (180).

595 For Ajax, see note on 307.

598 The QUEEN returns from the palace with the offerings she had promised at 523–24.

That when a wave of evils comes against a man,
He is likely to be afraid of everything thereafter;   600
But when the Spirit flows with gentle force, he trusts
The wind of lucky fortune always to blow the same.
For my part, everything has long been full of fear:
Both hostile visions from the gods have appeared to sight,
And a roaring—not a sound of healing—rings in my ears;   605
Such are the evils that stun and frighten me out of my wits.
Therefore I have retraced my steps from the house again
Without a chariot, without the former pomp,
Have come to bring to my son's father gracious gifts,
Libations such as soothe and mollify the dead: 610
The milk, so white and sweet to drink, of an unyoked cow,

599– *wave of evils:* (see note on 433); in *The Seven Against*
600 *Thebes* 758, the poet speaks of "a wave of troubles like the
sea." The QUEEN again indulges in generalizations, as in her
opening speech. She seems to be excusing what may appear
to be excessive fearfulness (cf. note on 603–606).

601– The case of the man who thinks his good luck will never run
602 out, although it completes the generalization, is not strictly
relevant to the QUEEN's point. It should be noted that
daimōn is used twice in these two lines, even though the
sense is "neutral" (cf. "Introduction," p. 15).

603– The QUEEN's fearful visions, the ringing in her ears, provide
606 an early and effective example of morbid psychology. She
has, as she implies, let the bad news get hold of her, has been
struck silly by it (606).

607– I take her words here as strong evidence that the QUEEN's
608 first appearance (159) was in a chariot, accompanied by a
fair amount of ostentatious pomp.

609 *gracious:* the word the CHORUS had used in their directions
to the QUEEN in 220 (cf. 685).

611– These are the usual offerings to the dead—but are they Per-
618 sian? What is unusual here, I believe, is the profusion and

77

And glowing honey, drops of flower-working bees,
Mixed in with drops of water from a virgin spring,
And, undefiled from its mother in the fields,
This drink, the radiant glory of an ancient vine;   615
And from the yellow olive always blossoming
In foliage the lovely scented fruit is here,
And woven garlands, offspring of the bountiful earth.
But friends, sing over these libations to the dead
Songs of good omen, and conjure up the Spirit of   620
Darius, while I send along their way these gifts
The earth will drink in honor to the gods below.

CHORUS   *O lady my Queen, whom the Persians revere,*

---

elaborateness with which they are catalogued. The QUEEN seems to be saying, "In my neurotic fear I brought everything I could think of." The adjectives emphasize purity, radiance, a kind of natural community of cow, bee, spring, and field. The offerings had to be perfect, ritually correct, or the discriminating dead might not respond. There is, moreover, the hint that all nature is related as so many children of earth, the Primeval Mother (see 614 and 618): vine, flower, cow, and bee—and man, living but especially dead—are all one.

620–
621
The command to conjure up the GHOST OF DARIUS comes as a slight surprise, but as well as being an effective theatrical stroke, it seems a logical development from the CHORUS' earlier advice to the QUEEN (220–22). The groundwork has been laid by the numerous references to the dead king (6, 145, 156, 160, 164, 198, 221, 244, 554), who has already, in the minds of the characters, begun to assume the role of "guardian spirit" to the royal house. (*Daimōn* in 620 seems to bear the semi-technical sense of a heroic figure, who, after death, is becoming a demigod.)

623–
632
An anapestic prelude again precedes the lyrics that begin at 633.

623
The CHORUS' address to the QUEEN is again marked by extreme respect; in Greek she is called, idiomatically, "reverence [i.e., object of reverence] to the Persians."

78

Send libations below to the halls underground,
While we with our songs shall beseech   625
The escorts of the dead
   To be gracious beneath the earth.

They turn from the QUEEN, and stretch out
their hands toward the ground.

But O holy Spirits of the nether world,
Lady Earth and Hermes, and the King of the Dead,
Send a soul from beneath to the light above;   630
If he knows some additional cure for our ills,
He alone might tell it to men.

STROPHE 1

Does he hear me? the blessed King equal to God,
   As I send my native cries
Shrill and varied and clear,   635
Woeful sorrowful shrieks?
Will my pitiful woes
Penetrate through?
Can he hear me then below?

625– They must make their request to the right gods, those
630 "chthonic holy spirits" (628), whom we discover to be
Earth and Hermes (to be "soul-escort" is one of Hermes'
ordinary functions in Greek myth) and the "King of
Corpses," i.e., Hades or Pluto (called Aidoneus at 649).

631– A hopeless jumble in the original; each commentator makes
632 his own guesses, and I have translated mine.

633– The CHORUS begins its incantations. (We are left to wonder
639 how much of what follows is "authentic," i.e., drawn from
contemporary Greek ghost-ritual, how much simply suitably
eerie and threatrically convincing.) Aeschylus was later to
achieve a similar effect in the scene in which Electra, Orestes,
and the Chorus ritually call upon Agamemnon's Spirit to
assist them in *The Libation Bearers* 315–509.

ANTISTROPHE 1

But you O Earth and others who lead the dead,   640
    Allow the Spirit to come
Proud from the halls below,
God born in Susa for Persians.
Send him up,
Whose like never yet   645
The Persian earth covered over.

STROPHE 2

Truly beloved was the man, dear is his tomb, dear the re-
    mains that it covers.
Aidoneus release,
Escort, Aidoneus,   650
Our peerless Lord Darius. Ai!

ANTISTROPHE 2

Never our men did he slay, never through deadly infatuate
    war.

640– Besides honoring DARIUS, the phrases suggest that he is a
646   worthy companion of these nether powers, that in releasing
     him they will merely be extending to an equal the courtesy
     he deserves.

643   *God born in Susa:* a clear reference to Persian worship of
     kings (see also 157, 634, 654–55, 711, and 856). The evidence
     is collected and discussed in Appendix I of Lily Ross Taylor's
     The Divinity of the Roman Emperor (American Philological
     Association Monograph 1, Middletown, Conn., 1931).

647– The CHORUS describes its deep affection for the dead king
651   and his "ways" (the translation refers to, conventionally and
     colorlessly, his *remains*), an affection that transfers itself
     even to his tomb. Hades is addressed under one of his other
     names, *Aidoneus.*

652– The CHORUS utters what is in fact a seditious and only thinly
656   veiled criticism of XERXES when they remark, pointedly, that

God's counselor was he called
For the Persians; God's counselor 655
He was, for he steered the army well. Ai!

STROPHE 3

Sultan, ancient
Sultan, come, appear!
Come to the topmost peak of the tomb
Raising your saffron-tinted slipper, 660
Showing the feathers
Of your royal tiara.
Come father unharming Darius. Oh!

"he [DARIUS] did not ever slay men with war-destroying acts of madness" (a fine, full Aeschylean phrase). The comparison, so unfavorable to XERXES, has already been hinted at (555-56) and will be reiterated (663).

654– A rare word (*theomēstōr*) is used twice to emphasize two
655 of DARIUS' characteristics: (1) his godliness and (2) the wisdom of his planning; *God's counselor* is my rendering. The term is close to the Homeric phrase, "counselor equal to the gods" (used about Priam, Patroclus, and Neleus), but the compound word has the effect of continuing the suggestion made repeatedly earlier in the ode that DARIUS has found his place among the gods; the wisdom of his counsel has been proven to be divine (cf. note on 643).

656 The image, steering a ship by means of the sheet, is the result of emendation, but one which is generally accepted.

657– The stanza opens with a double occurrence of a word, which,
663 according to the ancient lexicographer Hesychius, was the Phrygian term for "king." In any case, it would have had an exotic, oriental sound to a Greek ear. The exotic details continue: *slipper, feathers,* and *tiara* are all equivalents of Persian terms.

ANTISTROPHE 3

That you may hear
Sorrows new and strange,   665
Master of my master appear.
A kind of Stygian death-mist flutters;
For all the youth
Has already perished.   670
Come, father, unharming Darius. Oh!

EPODE

Aiai! Aiai!
O much bewept by friends in death
Why O master, master   675
This double and doubly lamented mistake?
For all this country's
Three-banked ships are lost,
Ships no longer ships.   680

664– This stanza echoes themes of the opening one: the CHORUS'
671 woes, will he hear them? The phrase in 666 suggests "Lord
     of lords." Broadhead aptly compares *Stygian death-mist* (the
     Styx, in Greek mythology, was the main river of the Under-
     world) with the miasmatic mist hovering over Orestes and
     his accursed house in *The Eumenides* 378–79.

672– The song ends with a single independent stanza, or *epode,*
680 as also at 897–906 and 1066–77: see "Metrical Schema."
     With no metrical equivalent for comparison, manuscript
     corruptions here are numerous and for the most part beyond
     remedy. At 674 the CHORUS' affection for DARIUS and the
     tears shed at his death are again mentioned, as at the begin-
     ning of Strophe 2.

676 I have translated Gilbert Murray's invented text; the *mis-*
     take (*hamartia*) may refer to the loss of men alluded to in
     669–70 and the destruction of the navy mentioned in the
     lines that follow.

679– Ships "with three sets of thole-pins," i.e., three-banked
680 triremes (repeated in 1075), are "unshipped, unshipped": a

DARIUS appears, costumed exotically as befits a
Persian king.

DARIUS *O men of greatest trust, companions of my youth,*
O aged Persians, what sorrow is it that grips the city?
It groans, the ground is struck and furrows made in it.
I look upon my wife who stands so near the tomb
And am afraid. The offerings I received were gracious,   685
But you who stand around my tomb now raise a dirge
And, shrilly wailing your laments to raise the dead,
You call upon me piteously. But the road is not
An easy one to take, and the gods beneath the earth
Especially are better at taking than releasing.   690
Nevertheless, I exercised authority there

---

rather extravagant example of a Greek, especially Euripidean,
idiom.

681– We have no way of knowing how long an interval there was
683 between the CHORUS' closing words and the appearance of
DARIUS. But the effect of the incantations was clearly to put
them—and the audience—in a trance-like state, and DARIUS'
appearance, when it comes, is meant to have an electric
effect on the onlookers. (In a modern Greek production in
the summer of 1965 the choral song was accompanied by
wild gyrations, reaching what was almost a pitch of ecstasy;
who is to say that the ancient audience did not respond with
the same feverish excitement as the modern one?)

681 *O men of greatest trust:* "Faithful among faithful" is closer
to the original and is, of course, a way of saying "faithful to
the most superlative degree," similar to "king of kings."

688– His ascent took some effort (*hic labor, hoc opus est,* as
689 Vergil wrote about ascent from the underworld), if only of
persuasion.

689– There is indeed, as Broadhead comments, "a grim sort of
690 humour in the statement."

691 "I was a dynast among them," the Greek says; i.e., "I was
in a position of royal authority there (as on earth)." In a

And came. Be quick; I'll not be blamed for tarrying.
What new and heavy evil weighs upon the Persians?

STROPHE

CHORUS *Reverently I shrink from looking,*
Reverently I shrink from speaking,   695
Because of ancient dread of you.

DARIUS *Now that I have come from Hades, yielding to*
your shrill laments,
Do not make a lengthy story, shorten what you have to say;
Speak and finish all the matter, casting off respect of me.

ANTISTROPHE

CHORUS *Fearfully I flee from complying,*   700

---

similar vein, the Chorus in *The Libation Bearers* addresses
the spirit of Agamemnon as "radiant reverend ruler beneath
the earth . . . for you were a king while you lived . . ."
(355–60).

692 This command to hurry is intended to characterize the
speaker as still a king, used to giving orders and having them
obeyed (the reason he gives adds a dignified touch).

693 The Greek contains a verbal suggestion of 346, where the
scales are weighted against the enemy.

694– Two short choral stanzas are here interrupted by three tro-
702 chaic tetrameters from DARIUS, after which the scene continues in trochaics between DARIUS and the QUEEN. The
verses are formulaic; verbal repetition is reinforced by rhyme
at line end within each stanza, and the words which end the
second line are the same in both stanzas.

The CHORUS addresses DARIUS as the king they had known
and revered.

698 Cf. 692 and note.

700f *Fearfully . . . Fearfully:* This refrain depends upon an

84

Fearfully I flee from speaking,
Words unutterable to friends.

DARIUS *Now that ancient fear has taken up its stand be-*
      fore your mind,
Lady, nobly born and aged, honored partner of my bed,
Take a respite from this weeping and these sighs and speak to
      me   705
Clearly: man's condition means that sufferings will come to
      men.
Many evil happenings from the sea, and many from the land
Come upon men, especially if they stretch their time of life
      too far.

      The QUEEN, who has been standing silently
      by, speaks.

---

      emended text, plausible if DARIUS' response at 696ff., like
      703, is to the CHORUS.

703 The image is of a guard "standing before" the mind—and so
      obstructing it—like an athletic opponent. The line may,
      however, be addressed to the QUEEN.

704 The elaborate formality of the address bespeaks the courtesy
      of the king to his wife, whom he postpones addressing until
      this point. With 705 contrast his earlier brusque commands
      to the CHORUS; and, for another kind of contrast, cf. the
      stiff formality of Agamemnon's address to Clytemnestra,
      when it finally comes, at *Agam.* 914ff.

706– A good example of the practice (characteristic of tragedy)
708 of extending a proverbial commonplace.

708 A long life allowed many changes of fortune, as Solon made
      clear to Croesus, and there was always the danger that the
      felicity of one's youth and middle age might be reversed by
      the inevitable ills of old age. Thus "call no man happy
      until he's dead," that most Greek of maxims, had a sound
      basis in geriatrics.

QUEEN *You who surpassed all other men in fortunate*
prosperity,
While you looked upon the rays of sun, how enviable you
  were,   710
Leading your life successfully among the Persians, like a God;
Now I also envy you your death before you saw defeat.
For, Darius, you shall hear the entire tale in brief account:
All the city-sacking Persian nation has itself been sacked.

DARIUS *How did it happen? Did some sudden plague*
  descend? Or a revolt?   715

QUEEN *No, not that; but the whole army was destroyed*
  near Athens' town.

DARIUS *Who of all my sons there drove the army into*
  battle? Speak.

---

709   The QUEEN had talked of the prosperity, *olbos*, of the royal
      house at 163–64, and she recurs to it both here and again
      at 756. In this context she couples it with *eutuchia*, "luck";
      elsewhere, the two are distinguished as (true) happiness
      versus (mere) luck (see, e.g., Herodotus 1. 32. 7).

711   *like a God*: cf. 157, 643, and "Introduction," p. 15.

713– The QUEEN complies with DARIUS' request to the CHORUS
714   (692, 698). There is a pun in the line: the word for "sack"
      and "Persian" share the same root in Greek (see note on
      178).

715   DARIUS thinks at once of the two most common catastrophes,
      plague and revolution (*stasis*). There was trouble over the
      succession when he ascended the throne (Herodotus 3. 73ff.),
      and a dispute again arose before he named a successor
      (7. 2, 3). The image is of a thunderbolt suddenly striking
      the city.

717   DARIUS had seven sons (three by a former wife, the daughter
      of Gobryas, before he became king, four by Atossa after-
      wards: Herodotus 7. 2), any of whom could have been the

QUEEN *Furious Xerxes, who emptied out the whole,*
broad-stretching continent.

DARIUS *How did he make this foolish venture, wretched*
man—on foot?—by sea?

QUEEN *Both of them. His double armament had both*
appearances.   720

DARIUS *How did such an enormous army manage to get*
across on foot?

QUEEN *Cunningly he yoked the strait of Helle so it held*
a road.

DARIUS *This did he contrive, so that he fastened shut*
great Bosporus?

QUEEN *Yes, he did. But I suppose some Spirit aided in*
his plan.

---

one in question here; but the right of succession was secured
for XERXES before DARIUS' death (Atossa's doing, according
to Herodotus 7. 3: "she had all the power").

718 *Furious:* cf. notes on 73 and 754. Here it may suggest his
impetuosity.

720 The Greek says the expedition had two "faces" (like a
double herm or single bust with two heads, back to back).

722 A reference to the bridge of boats across the Hellespont; cf.
113–14 which may also refer to the bridge, and note on 70–71.

723 *Bosporus:* occasionally used by the Greeks as a synonym for
"Hellespont." The line ignores the story, reported later by
Herodotus (4. 83), that DARIUS himself performed a similar
feat in bridging the Thracian Bosporus preparatory to his
invasion of Scythia. In Herodotus' version, XERXES was even
reminded that disaster followed when DARIUS bridged the
Thracian Bosporus (7. 10).

724– The lines are crucial to an understanding of XERXES' personal
725   tragedy. It is not accidental that the phrasing of 725, *Some*

DARIUS *Ah! Some powerful Spirit must have come to take away his wits.* 725

QUEEN *So much so that the evil end which he accomplished can be seen.*

DARIUS *What is the evil fate the men met that you make such loud lament?*

QUEEN *Once the navy met disaster, all the infantry was lost.*

DARIUS *So the whole armed troop has been completely ruined by the spear?*

QUEEN *For this reason all of Susa groans for its emptiness of men.* 730

DARIUS *O for the loss of staunch support, the strong defense the army gave!*

QUEEN *Bactrians, too, went to defeat; their men were utterly destroyed.*

DARIUS *Pitiful creature, how youthful was the force of allies he destroyed!*

QUEEN *Only Xerxes, all alone they say, and not with many men—*

---

powerful Spirit [*daimōn*] *must have come* . . . is reminiscent of the MESSENGER's account of the beginning of the Salamis fiasco.

726– The QUEEN reveals details only gradually, as is the custom
728 in this kind of "stichomythia" (line-by-line exchange). Line 728 is directly echoed by Herodotus, who puts an almost identical phrase in the mouth of Queen Artemisia of Halicarnassus (8. 68, before Salamis).

729– The two themes, the symbolic Greek spear and the city
730 grieving for its *emptiness of men,* are reiterated.

732 The end of this line as given in the manuscripts is corrupt beyond remedy.

DARIUS How and where did he reach his end? Or was
there yet some means of escape? 735

QUEEN Glad was he to come at last to the bridge that
yoked two continents.

DARIUS Did he really manage to get back in safety to this
side?

QUEEN Yes, this story clearly wins the day, and there is
no dispute.

DARIUS Ah! The working out of oracles has come, and
swiftly too!
Zeus hurled down against my son accomplishment of prophecies; 740

---

736 *continents:* translates a standard emendation, but another
proposed emendation would render "the bridge, a single
yoke of two." This statement conflicts with Herodotus' version, where XERXES returns to find the bridges broken up by
a storm and crosses with the army to Abydos on ships (8.
117). Both of these versions are less likely than the third
story, rejected by Herodotus, that XERXES left the army at
Eion on the Strymon River and was carried back to Asia
with a group of Persian grandees on a Phoenician ship (8.
118). Obviously there were differing accounts of how
XERXES made the last leg of his return journey (*vid.* 738).
Aeschylus' version, whether true or not, has the dramatic
advantage of isolating XERXES.

738 *dispute* (*stasis*): echoes the earlier occurrences of the word
(188 and 715). The connotation of political discontent is
reinforced by the presence in the same line of *wins* (*kratei*)
another "political" word. The line implies that there was
some doubt, even in 472 B.C., concerning the exact method
of XERXES' crossing.

739– This reference to oracles foretelling the disaster for Persia
741 but leaving the time of fulfillment open is a new and unexpected element in the story, but one that contributes

*I was confident the gods would work them out in distant
    time:*
*But, whenever a man himself goes rushing in, God speeds
    him on.*
*Now it seems a fountain of disaster was found for all our
    friends.*
*This is what my son accomplished, blindly, with impetuous
    youth,*
*He who hoped to check the flow of sacred Hellespont with
    bonds,*   745

---

significantly to the supernatural atmosphere of the tragedy.
It is a favorite motif in Herodotus: the fall of the Mermnad
dynasty in Lydia was foretold by Delphi "in the fifth generation" (1. 13); even Apollo could not put off the fall of Sardis
to Croesus' descendants, although he tricked the Fates into
deferring it for three years (1. 91).

742 A cardinal tenet of Aeschylean theology; cf. 724 and note.

743 Compare the "silver springs" of 238.

744 The implications of XERXES' epithets, "wild" and "furious"
     (73, 718, and 754), are here made explicit. He acted with
     youthful rashness and in ignorance.

745– The sacrilege is emphasized in the language: the Hellespont
748   (here called "Bosporus" again) was "holy" and a stream
      sacred to God; XERXES attempted to shackle it like a common
      slave and to change its form. Herein precisely lay his main
      offense from a ritualistic point of view (and this is symbolic
      of an attitude of mind). More than merely the ancient taboo
      about bridging water is involved here; in trying to make a
      solid roadway on water, XERXES was tampering with nature
      and so, implicitly, violating God's will. With the *Ham-
      mered chains* of 748 (perhaps iron anchors and their
      cables), compare the story of XERXES' flogging of the
      Hellespont and his letting chains down into it in insensate
      fury (Herodotus 7. 35). According to Herodotus, he uttered
      the words: "Harsh water, your master inflicts this just
      penalty, because you did an injustice to him [in allowing
      the first set of bridges to be destroyed by a storm] although

Shackled like some slave the Bosporus, the holy spring of
    God.
Forcing his route to take a shape against its nature and cast-
    ing on
Hammered chains, he managed to make a road to match his
    mass of men.
Mortal that he was he foolishly thought that he could master
    all
Gods, among them Poseidon. Surely this was some disease
    of mind   750
Gripping him? I fear that the vast wealth I labored for is
    gone,
Overturned, left for the taking of anyone who comes along.

    QUEEN   Evil were the men who taught him and he
           learned his lesson well,

---

you suffered no injustice at his hands. And King XERXES
will cross you, whether you will it or no." Some of this
characterization seems to derive from hints in Aeschylus'
portrait of the king.

749– The human/divine levels here cross—unnaturally and dis-
750 astrously. XERXES had delusions of grandeur, aspirations to
divinity (perhaps an attempt to match his father). The lines
give very much the same impression as his megalomaniac
outburst quoted in the preceding note. His folly is a species
of insanity, "disease of mind" (i.e., mental illness).

751 *wealth*: compare 163, 168, 237, 250, 755, and 842.

753– It has not generally been noticed that a very similar motif
758 is used of DARIUS, this time with the QUEEN herself as
temptress: "It is fitting for you," Herodotus has Atossa say
at the beginning of DARIUS' reign, "so young a man and
master of such wealth, to make a show of your power, so
that the Persians may learn that they are ruled by a *man* and,
being occupied with a war, will not have time to conspire
against you. Now is the time to make a display, when you
are young . . ." (3. 134). It may be that Herodotus has
borrowed from Aeschylus but transferred the story to an

Furious Xerxes. You, they said, by fighting got enormous
    wealth,
Left it to your children; while your son, through lack of man-
    liness,   755
Cast his spear indoors, did not increase the prosperity you
    left.
Hearing such reproaches often on the lips of evil men
This was the expedition he devised and led his troops to
    Greece.

DARIUS And so a deed has been accomplished by him
    now,
So great and unforgettable, such as never yet   760
Had brought to this citadel of Susa—emptiness,
Since first Lord Zeus bestowed on us this honored rule:
That a single man should hold the whole of Asia, nurse
Of flocks, in sceptered sway and dictate all its laws.
For Medos was the first to lead our mass of men: 765

---

earlier generation, although the theme of "evil companions"
recurs in Herodotus' story of XERXES (7. 15).

754– Another new element in the story, which increases our sym-
756 pathy for XERXES. Under such goading, how could he fail to
respond with a daring and extravagant, but foolish, venture?

759ff Cf. "Metrical Schema."

759– The adjectives are purposely ambiguous; we do not know
760 until 761 that their force is ironical.

763– "Sheep-nurturing" seems to have been a traditional epithet
764 for Asia (Archilochus, fragment 23, Diehl).

765– DARIUS gives a thumbnail history of the early Median and
780 Persian kings. The list cannot be squared in many details
with either Herodotus' account or the Behistun inscription
of DARIUS, and attempts at reconciliation are probably mis-
guided. For a Greek, the history of Media-Persia was largely
legendary.

765 I take *Medos* to be a mythical, eponymous ancestor of the

Another, who was his son, also accomplished this.
The third in line of descent was Cyrus, blessed of men,   (768)
Who, as he ruled, established peace for all his friends.   (769)
For with his mind he steered the tiller of his heart.   (767)
The people of Lydia and Phrygia he acquired,   770
And all Ionia he forcibly subdued.
For God did not begrudge his rule, so wise was he.
The son of Cyrus was the fourth to direct the host.
And fifth to rule was Mardos, a disgrace to country
And to his ancient throne. With guile he was slain   775
By noble Artaphrenes in the royal halls,
With many friends who took this deed upon themselves,
[The sixth was Maraphis, the seventh Artaphrenes]
By me myself. The lot then fell as I had wished.
And I led numerous campaigns with many men,   780
But never brought so much disaster on the city.

---

royal house, but it may be that Aeschylus simply meant "a Mede." In that case 765 may refer to Cyaxares, 766 to Astyages.

768 Cyrus is called *eudaimōn*, "possessed of supernatural good fortune" (or, more simply, "blessed"). He was one of the truly fabulous rulers of the East in the eyes of the Greeks; his people called him "gentle father, because he devised all sorts of benefits for them" (Herodotus 3. 89). His career is recounted at length by Herodotus.

767 This line seems appropriate to Cyrus; hence the transposition (after Page and Broadhead).

772 Again, a contrast with XERXES: God did not hate him.

778 The line has been bracketed and may not be genuine, although it is difficult to offer reasons for its insertion. These names are omitted in other accounts, but see note on 765–780.

779 That is, he obtained the crown—how it was done is narrated in Herodotus 3. 73–87. The "lot" was really the preplanned whinny of DARIUS' horse!

Yet Xerxes my son is young in years and young in mind,
And he does not remember what my instructions were.
For you are well aware of this, my friends in age,
That all of us who ever held this royal power   785
Would not have caused so many manifest sufferings.

CHORUS   O lord Darius, where and to what end do you
turn
Your words? How could we, the people of Persia, still
Retrieve good fortune, now that matters stand this way?

DARIUS   If you do not campaign against the land of
Greece,   790
And if there is no further Persian expedition:
For their land itself fights as an ally with them.

CHORUS   What do you mean by this? How does it fight
with them?

DARIUS   By starving to death invaders whose numbers are
too great.

CHORUS   Yes, but we shall raise a fine, selected force.   795

DARIUS   No, even the army waiting now in Greek terrain
Will never reach again the safety of return.

CHORUS   What are you saying? All the Persian army
won't
Return again across the strait of Helle from Europe?

---

782   XERXES' youth is doubly emphasized, with an implication of
rashness in "young thoughts." The words may be proverbial.

787–   The CHORUS pragmatically brings matters back to the present
789   and asks for advice.

790–   Aeschylus and his audience probably hoped that the Persians
791   would heed DARIUS' warning.

792–   In Herodotus (7. 49) XERXES is warned by his uncle, Arta-
794   banus, that "the land is your enemy" (because of the difficulty of obtaining provisions for so large a force so far from
home).

DARIUS A few from many, if one must put his trust in the
    gods'   800
Prophetic statements, as he looks upon what now
Has happened: for prophecies stop not at half-fulfillment.
If this is so, Xerxes leaves a hand-picked mass
Of troops in vain, yielding to his empty hopes.
They wait where Asopus with his streams waters the plain   805
And brings a welcome richness to the Boeotian land.
The crown of wretched suffering awaits them there,
Requital for their hybris and their godless thoughts.
They went to the land of Greece and did not scruple to
    strip

796– This is the first we hear of the picked force left with
797   Mardonius (300,000 men, according to Herodotus 8. 113);
        contrast 482–84. DARIUS had not known of the expedition in
        the first place (715) but is now able prophetically to foretell
        disaster for a large part of it: cf. 739, 800–2.

805– The scene described is Plataea, near Thebes, where Mar-
806   donius' army was decisively beaten by the Greeks in the
        summer of 479 B.C.

808– I have kept the Greek term hybris here and in 821. There
812   is no adequate English term to describe the attitude of mind
        and the actions which resulted from it by which a human
        indulged his "delusions of grandeur," refusing to accept the
        limitations of his mortality and so risking divine "jealousy"
        (see 362 and compare 772). The term is applied to both
        XERXES and his army.

      A new element is here introduced: the Persians' godless
attitude manifests itself in specific acts of irreligion. The
reference is primarily to the burning of temples in Attica,
chief among them those on the Acropolis (Herodotus 8. 53–
54), but there were other shrines destroyed en route (as in
Phocis, Herodotus 8.32). Compare the sentiments ascribed
by Herodotus to Themistocles (8. 109. 3); I suggest that
what we have here may be a genuine echo of these (see
further, my Political Background, pages 21–23).

The images of the gods, set fire to their temples.   810
For altars were destroyed, and shrines of the gods pried up
From their foundations and strewn about in complete
    confusion.
Therefore, since they acted evilly, they suffer
No less evilly in turn, will suffer more;
The foundation rests: the edifice is not yet built.   815
So great will be the flow of bloody gore from wounds
In the land of the Plataeans by the Dorian spear.
And heaps of corpses even generations hence
Will signify in silence to the eyes of men
That mortal man should not think more than mortal

811– The vigorous language reflects the violence of the act (cf.
812   163 and note). The wording of 811 is closely paralleled by
      Agamemnon 527 and the latter has therefore been con-
      demned by some editors. But the situations are similar, and
      who is to say a poet cannot repeat himself?

813– This law, that the "doer must suffer," that each sinful act
814   creates a kind of cosmic imbalance which must be restored,
      is exemplified repeatedly in Aeschylus' trilogy, the *Oresteia*.

815 The manuscripts give an entirely different sense: "The
     foundation of evils is not yet laid." But what we really want
     is "*only* the foundation is thus far laid (there is more to
     come)." None of the suggested emendations gives this sense,
     and most of them radically alter the imagery as well as re-
     quiring drastic rewriting of the Greek.

817 See note on 805. Is Aeschylus emphasizing Plataea as a
     specifically Dorian (i.e., Spartan) victory, as most commenta-
     tors think? The robes of one of the women in the QUEEN's
     dream are called "Doric" (183); clearly nothing more than
     an equivalent of "Greek" was intended, and it is possible
     that that is the meaning here.

818 A grimly appropriate conception, a ritualistic way of saying
     "forever." Herodotus reports that after the battle, "the
     corpses were bare of flesh; the Plataeans collected the bones
     in one place" (8. 83).

thoughts. 820
For hybris blossomed forth and grew a crop of ruin,
And from it gathered in a harvest full of tears.
As you look upon these deeds and recompense for them,
Remember Athens and Greece and let no man hereafter,
Despising what he has from heaven, turn lustful eyes 825
To others, and spill a store of great prosperity.
For Zeus is standing by, the punisher of thoughts
Too overboastful, a harsh and careful scrutineer.
In face of this, when Xerxes, who lacks good sense, returns,
Counsel him with reasoning and good advice, 830
To cease from wounding God with overboastful rashness.

DARIUS turns to address the QUEEN.

And you, Xerxes' aged mother, dear to him,

---

820 This is the moral of XERXES' story, succinctly stated.

824 This line in its pregnant context may have inspired the
anecdote told by Herodotus and applied to DARIUS (cf. note
on 285).

825 The Greek says, "despising the present *daimōn*." (On
daimōn, see "Introduction," pp. 14-16).
lustful eyes: perhaps overtranslates what is, however, a
basically erotic word.

826 Here the image is varied slightly; perhaps it is of an overturned pitcher of wine or sack of grain.

827- The moralizing tone grows more insistent; cf. the Athenian
828 practice of scrutinizing a magistrate's records after his tenure
of office.

829 *lacks good sense*: can only with difficulty be extracted from
the Greek as it stands.

830 For the CHORUS' role as venerable counselors, cf. 170-72.

831 *wounding God*: the verb (*theoblabeō*) in an active sense
was probably invented by Aeschylus and seems to have been
imitated by Euripides in *The Bacchae* as "to God-fight"
(*theomacheō*).

Go into the house and take whatever robe
Is most becoming and go to meet your son; for his
Attire all around his body is in shreds,   835
And his embroidered robes are torn through with grief.
But you now calm and soothe him using kindly words:
For only you, I know, will he bear to listen to.
But I am returning underneath the gloom of earth.
And you farewell, Elders; even in disaster   840
Allow your spirits to indulge in daily joys,
For wealth is not of any use at all to the dead.

      DARIUS departs.

   CHORUS *Many, indeed, are the sufferings both present and yet*
To come for us that I listened to and grieved to hear.

    QUEEN *O Spirit! How many grievous sufferings have* 845
     come
Upon me, but this misfortune stings me most of all,
To hear of the dishonor that attends my son
In having to wear about his person tattered clothes.

833– This has been thought an expedient to get the QUEEN off the
836   stage and allow the actor in her part to adopt the role of
    XERXES. But the QUEEN's departure serves an essentially
    dramatic purpose: XERXES must be allowed to have the center
    of grief (and blame) to himself at the end.

842   The theme of wealth (*ploutos*) is brought to an end on a
    very personal note.

845– The QUEEN once more addresses the *daimōn*. Some critics
851   have viewed the speech as absurd and therefore spurious.
    There is, however, nothing unAeschylean in the language
    and the absurdity disappears once we appreciate the sym-
    bolic value of the king's attire (see "Introduction," p. 3,
    note 1).

846   Persian emphasis on ceremonial dress to denote rank meant
    that its loss also denoted loss of rank. Greek attitude and
    usage were otherwise, and more like ours.

But *I* am going, and *I* shall bring from out of the house
A robe, and *I* shall try to meet him on the way.   850
For we shall not betray our dear ones in these troubles.

STROPHE 1

CHORUS   Oh, oh, great, indeed, and good was the life
Of civil law and order that we had,
When the aged King,
All-sufficing, bringing no harm, invincible   855
Darius equal to God
Ruled the land.

ANTISTROPHE 1

First, the armed forces we showed to the world
Were honored, and attacked the citadels
Of foes lawfully.   860

852– See "Metrical Schema." In this choral song, the elders long
908   for a return to their nation's glorious past, the idealized
      "golden age" of DARIUS' rule.

853   *civil law and order*: a Greek, rather than Persian, concept.

854– Each adjective enhances DARIUS' image. With *no harm*
856   compare 555, 652–53, 663, 671; *invincible* ignores the
      abortive Scythian campaign and Marathon; and *equal to
      God* in a climactic position, recalls 634, 643, and 711. It is
      an idealized portrait of the former king, and one designed
      to contrast with the sufferings which XERXES has brought
      upon his subjects.

858   From the personal excellence of their former king, they pass
      to the glorious reputation once possessed by their armies.

859– No emendation of the obvious textual corruption is really
860   convincing, but an ancient note seems to point to a distinc-
      tion between a lawful mode of behavior under DARIUS and
      an implied unlawful one under XERXES.
         attacked: based on a suggestion of Sidgwick's.

Back from wars, suffering no harm, uninjured
They returned again
Successfully home.

STROPHE 2

How many cities he captured without ever crossing the Halys, 865
Not even stirring from home!
The Acheloian towns that neighbor on the Strymon
And the Thracian regions,   870

ANTISTROPHE 2

And the ones outside the lake on the mainland, surrounded
        by towers,
Listened to him as their lord,
Those near the broad stream of Helle, and serried Propontis, 875
And the mouths of Pontus.

861– Another contrast with the huge losses of XERXES' campaign
863   (255, 800) and the horrors of the journey home (482–511).

865   Here begins a proud catalogue of the cities of the empire once
       ruled over by Persia, now lost.

865– The ease of DARIUS' conquests is emphasized, in fact, exag-
866   gerated. To the Greeks, the Halys River was the western
       boundary of Persia; DARIUS added to the empire without, in
       effect, having to lift a finger.

867– A catalogue of geographical names similar to those found
894   elsewhere in Aeschylus (above, 485–95 with note): first the
       mainland cities in or near Thrace, with a list of the island
       dominions from 880 on.

869   Acheloian . . . Strymon: What cities are meant is uncertain,
       perhaps the towns built in the fresh-water Lake Prasias
       (Herodotus 5. 16); for the Strymon River see 497.

875   The CHORUS proceeds eastward, mentioning in geographical
       order the cities on the west coast of the Hellespont (stream
       of Helle), the Propontis (Sea of Marmara), with its curving
       and indented coastline, and the Thracian Bosporus.

STROPHE 3

And islands, washed by the sea near the headland   880
Located near this land,
Like Lesbos and Samos, where olives grow,
Chios and Paros, Naxos, Myconos,
And Andros, the adjacent   885
Neighbor to Tenos.

ANTISTROPHE 3

And he ruled over those out to sea from the mainland,
Lemnos and Icaros   890
And Rhodes and Cnidos and the towns of Cyprus,
Paphos and Soli and Salamis,
Whose mother-city is the cause   895
Of these laments.

EPODE

And the wealthy populous cities

---

880   The CHORUS turns to the islands, most of which (with the
      probable exception of Cyprus in lines 893-94) will by now
      (472 B.C.) have joined Athens' maritime league: Persia's
      loss was Athens' gain.

882-   The first three islands named are the largest and most im-
886   portant and are closest to the shore of Ionia. The CHORUS
      proceeds westward, mentioning five islands in the group
      known as the "Cyclades" (because they circle around Delos).

890-   Of the first four islands named in this stanza, only Rhodes,
892   which lies off the southwest coast of Asia Minor, was of any
      importance. According to Herodotus, Cyprus' struggle for
      independence was hard fought (as was its resistance in
      World War II).

893-   The three towns of Cyprus are enumerated, culminating in
894   Salamis—which allows another reference to its name-sake on
      the Greek mainland.

897ff A short concluding stanza, which summarizes the main

Of Greeks in the Ionian land
He ruled in his wisdom.　　　　　　　　　　　　900
The unwearying strength
Of warrior men and manifold allies
Was at hand.
But now the reversal of this we endure:
God has turned it around without doubt;　　　　905
We were overwhelmed
And stricken greatly at sea.

　　　XERXES enters in a chariot, his robes dirty and
　　　torn from the hasty retreat.

　　XERXES　*Oh! wretched am I, for this horrible fate*
That I met gave no sign of what was to come.　　　910

---

themes and contrasts: the wealth of the Persian dominions, the vast number of men they controlled, and the strength they provided; the intelligence of DARIUS' rule; the definiteness of the disaster and its divine origin; the fact that it was basically a naval defeat (Salamis again).

908– This is the scene to which the whole play has been building,
1076 the pathetic appearance of the crushed and humiliated king, who has dominated the play up to now, we almost want to say, by his absence. And yet, it is the hardest scene in the play for a modern reader to appreciate, mainly because it is highly lyrical and elaborately stylized. There is little content to hold our attention; it is simply a prolonged *thrēnos,* or formal lament, in which king and CHORUS sing at length, cantata fashion, of the depth of their defeat: a Greek *de Profundis.* The music, the dance rhythms (cf. 1073)—in short, the performance—are lost. What is left is often hardly intelligible to a reader and can sometimes not even be translated (as, for example, the frequent and highly formal outbursts, exclamations, and cries of lament; a brave modern producer might try simply reproducing the Greek sounds).

910 *gave no sign:* DARIUS had mentioned threatening oracles (740, 801), only to make clear that he himself did not realize their applicability to XERXES.

102

How the Spirit came down on the Persian race
With savage intent! What am I to do
In my misery? For the strength of my limbs
Is gone as I see these citizens here.
O Zeus, I, too, should have died with men   915
Who are gone,
> *Covered over by Doom of Death.*

CHORUS   *Oh oh oh, King, Oh for the noble troops,*
And great honor of Persian rule,
And the glorious men,   920
Whom the Spirit has now mowed down.
The land cries aloud for the youth
Of the land whom Xerxes has slain
And stuffed into Hades. For many are they
From Agdabata-town, flower of the land,   925

911– Once again the *daimōn*, or Spirit, is invoked (see "Introduc-
912   tion," pp. 14–16).

913   The king's loss of strength in his limbs is an inward manifes-
      tation of his loss of royal power through loss of men (cf. 589–
      90, 928).

915– *men . . . gone:* Compare the opening line of the play (and
916   see note there).

917   *Doom of Death* is Homeric.

919   *great honor . . . rule:* The CHORUS earlier had lamented the
      fact that people were *ruled / No longer by Persian laws*
      (584–85); this is the *national* aspect of the tragedy.

921   Cf. 911.

922– "The land cries 'ai ai' for its own youth": compare the
923   land's longing for her own at 62 and again at 512.

923– XERXES is called, with extreme harshness, "stuffer of Hades
924   with Persians."

924– There is some doubt about these men of Agdabata. That it is
925   the name of some locality is the merest guess; the ancient
      Scholiast took it for the name of an ancient tribe. The word
      has an authentic Persian formation.

Who were slain by the bow, a forest of men,
Thousands on thousands destroyed.
Ah, ah, the noble might!
And the land of Asia, O King,
Has terribly, terribly sunk to her knees. 930

STROPHE 1

XERXES *I am here, oh oh, to be met with cries,*
Wretched, and, as it turns out, an evil
Both to my race and the land of my fathers.

CHORUS *To greet your return, I shall send up, up* 935
An evil-omened cry, the evil-boding shriek
Of a Mariandynian mourner,
A howl full of tears. 940

ANTISTROPHE 1

XERXES *Let loose your voice full of woe and lament,*

---

926 *the bow:* (here Greek) compare 460–61 and contrast 85–86
and 147–48.

926f Literally, "a very thick [dense] ten thousand."

930 The image had been used by Solon (fragment 4, Diehl) re-
garding *Athens:* "the Ionian land is bent to her knees." It
would not have been beyond an Athenian audience to detect
the reference and the irony of its application to Athens'
enemy.

933– This much is requisite for the tragic effect, that the victim
934 of disaster recognize his own share in his downfall.

935– The CHORUS does nothing to comply with the QUEEN's re-
936 quest earlier that they "comfort" the returning king (530),
or with DARIUS' command to *Counsel him with reasoning*
and good advice (830).

939 "The Mariandyni, a tribe that lived in the northern part of
Bithynia, near the Euxine, were noted for their dirges"
(Broadhead). Compare *The Libation Bearers* 423–24, "strains
of a Cissian mourning woman."

A wail of grief. For the Spirit has veered
And now turned his blast on me.

CHORUS *I shall let loose, then, a voice of lament,*
Feeling awe before the sorrows suffered at sea,   945
By the city that mourns her sons.
I shall peal out a tearful wail.

STROPHE 2

XERXES *The Ionians reaped,*   950
The Ionian warships
Turned the tide,
Cut a swathe through the night-dark sea
And the haunted shore.

---

942 *Spirit:* see 911–12 and "Introduction."
       veered: The Greek says simply "turned," but as parallel
       passages make clear, the image is of a sudden and destruc-
       tive shift in the wind.

945– Little sense can be made of the Greek. The translation pre-
946 supposes transposition of the compounds in 945 (see 275–
       77).

947 The verb, whose root is *klang-,* is used of any sharp, metallic
       sound, as of bells (*The Seven Against Thebes* 386). Its sound,
       therefore, suggests the meaning (onomatopoeia).

950– I accept Broadhead's interpretation of this rather cryptic
961 stanza, which, translated literally, is: "the Ares [= armed
       might; see note on 86], armed with ships, turning the balance
       of strength, which belonged to the Ionians, took away [vic-
       tory?; the object is not expressed], after it had cut through
       the night-dark surface [of sea] and the shore of-unlucky-
       daimōn." "Ionian" here stands for "Greek" (as at 178, 563,
       1011, 1025), and in Solon for "Athenian" (note on 930); the
       converse, "Hellene" for "Ionian," at 900. Is it an attempt
       to absolve the Ionians for their share in the fighting on the
       Persian side (see notes on 42, 178, and 1025)?

CHORUS   *Oh oh! Cry oh, and learn to the full.*   955
Where is the rest of the throng of friends?
Where are those who stood by you?
Men like Pharandakes,
Sousas, Pelagon, and Agabatas,
Psammis, Dotamas, and Sousiskanes,   960
Who set out from Ecbatana?

ANTISTROPHE 2

XERXES   *I left them behind,*
From a Tyrian warship
Gone to death,
On the shores of Salamis, striking   965
Against rock-hard coast.

CHORUS   *Oh oh! Cry oh; where did you leave*
Pharnouchos, and good Ariomardos?

955– H. J. Rose in his *Commentary* suggests that "this passage
961 [as well as 967–73] is easiest to understand if we suppose
that different members of the CHORUS sing each a line or
two."

958– "Of the names given in this strophe, five, according to Keiper,
960 are Persian, Pelagon is Greek, Psammis Egyptian" (Broadhead). Pharandakes and Sousiskanes were mentioned in the
entrance song (31, 34).

963 *Tyrian:* probably stands for "Phoenician." Under an earlier
king, "the whole naval part of the Persian armament de-
pended on the Phoenicians" (Herodotus 3. 19), who fur-
nished three hundred ships to XERXES' navy (7. 89).

967– "Of the nine names in this antistrophe five are undoubtedly
973 Persian (Pharnouchos, Ariomardos, Masistras, Artembares,
Hystaichmas), one (Lilaios) is Greek, Seualkes prob. Greek
(so Keiper), Memphis Egyptian, Tharybis doubtful" (Broadhead). For Pharnouchos, cf. 313; Ariomardos, 38, 321;
Lilaios, 308; Tharybis 51, 323; Masistras, 30; Artembares, 29,
302 (H. J. Rose).

Where is Lord Seualkes,
Lilaios the noble,   970
Memphis, Tharybis, and Masistras,
Artembares and Hystaichmas?
I ask you this again.

STROPHE 3

XERXES *Oh oh oh*
As soon as they saw ancient and hateful   975
Athens all at one stroke, ah!
They pitifully gasped on the shore.

CHORUS *And the flower of Persians,*
Your completely trustworthy eye,
The one who counted the tens of thousands,   980

---

976   *at one stroke:* The Greek word suggests the splash of oars
      dipping into water or wine splashing into a cup. It reminds
      the audience again that the disaster took place at sea.

977   Broadhead cites Herodotus 9. 120 for the image, "a vivid
      picture of the Persians, who, as they are washed up on shore,
      gasp for breath like the dying fish in a net."

978   *flower:* D. L. Page's emendation (cf. 252).

979   *trustworthy eye:* may be a reference to the Persian office of
      "Eye of the King," applied to "overseers" whose function
      was to inspect the provinces, or "satrapies," of the empire
      and report any signs of disaffection.

980   For the numbering of the army by tens of thousands, see
      302, 314, 993, and note on 304.

980– This section is a specimen of Aeschylus' careful interweaving
993   of repeated words and motifs. "Ten thousand," twice re-
      peated in the Greek of 980, is echoed in *Marshal of ten*
      thousand in 993. In between there is *Evils on evils you*
      tell at 986, picked up by *you speak of hateful evils on*
      evils in a parallel position at the end of 990. XERXES says
      at 988–89, *you remind me / Of love and longing* (literally,

Alpistos son of Batanochos

. . . .

Son of Sesames, son of Megabates,
And Parthos and Great Oibares—
Did you leave them behind? Oh oh, poor wretches.　　　　985
Evils on evils you tell for noble Persians.

ANTISTROPHE 3

XERXES *Yes, you remind me*
Of love and longing for noble comrades,
As you speak of hateful evils on evils;　　　　990
My heart screams within my limbs.

CHORUS *And others we long for,*
Marshal of ten thousand Mardoi,
Xanthes, and Anchares of the Arioi,
Diaixis and also Arsakes,　　　　995
Cavalry lords,
And Agdadates and Lythimnes,
And Tolmos insatiable in battle.

"of my love charm"), and the CHORUS begins its response
with *And others we long for* (992).

982　A line, corresponding to 996 in the antistrophe, has been
　　　lost.

991　If the interpretation is correct, it is a strong image; our phrase
　　　"in my breast" is rather pale by comparison.

993　See Herodotus 1. 125 for the nomadic Mardoi.

994　*of the Arioi:* Wilamowitz' emendation; the manuscripts give
　　　"warlike." (A similar manuscript reading has likewise been
　　　emended to "Arian" at *Choeph.* 423.) Herodotus says that
　　　"Arioi" was the original name of the Medes, "until Medea
　　　came from Colchis," 7. 62; they appear as a contingent in the
　　　Persian army, 7. 66.

997　*Agdadates* The manuscripts give several versions of the first,
　　　suitably Persian-sounding, name.

999　The Greek is more vigorous: "insatiate of the spear."

I am amazed—they are not in your train,　　　　　　1000
Do not follow behind your wheeled and curtained carriage.

STROPHE 4

XERXES *They have gone, those captains of the troops.*

CHORUS *They have gone, oh, unnamed.*

XERXES *Ah ah! Oh oh!*

CHORUS *Oh oh, Spirits!*　　　　　　　　　　　　1005
You have brought unexpected disaster.
How piercingly clear is the glance of Ruin!

ANTISTROPHE 4

XERXES *We are struck; what chance has struck our lives!*

1000– These lines have been taken by some scholars, including
1001 Broadhead, to indicate that XERXES actually appears on-
stage in this vehicle, called by Herodotus a *harmamaxa*
(7. 41). Herodotus reports that XERXES used it and his
chariot (*harma*) alternately on the way to Greece. It was
the usual mode of conveyance of wealthy Persian officials
(Plutarch, *Life of Themistocles* 26. 3); the "wheel-driven
tent," as the Greek phrase has it, had curtained hangings
which afforded shade and privacy. That XERXES should
appear in this, and at the same time in tatters, may strike
some as incongruous. Rose interprets the lines: "Not only
has XERXES no guardsmen attending his carriage, but there
is no carriage for them to attend."

1002f *They have gone:* See notes on 1, 13, 916.

1003 They are nameless in that they are now nothing but names,
and tens of thousands not even that.

1005 *Spirits:* see "Introduction," pp. 14–16.

1006– There is some disturbance in the text, but the translation
1007 renders the probable image. Compare *unexpected disaster*
with 265.

1008 The translation is a makeshift for the meaningless Greek
phrase "throughout (our) lifetime."

CHORUS *We are struck, as can be seen.*

XERXES *With new pain, new pain.*   1010

CHORUS *Ionian sailors*
We encountered unluckily;
Luckless in war is the race of Persians.

STROPHE 5

XERXES *Of course it is. I felt the blow that was struck*
At so huge an army.   1015

CHORUS *What part of the Persians survives, man of*
      sorrows?

XERXES *You see what is left of my troops?*

CHORUS *I see, I see.*

XERXES *And this arrow-holding . . .*   1020

CHORUS *What is this you say was saved?*

XERXES *Storehouse for the shafts?*

CHORUS *Little enough from much.*

XERXES *We are stripped of our defenders.*

CHORUS *The Ionian host does not run from battle.*   1025

1011 See note on 950–61.

1014– The king's formulation suggests that he considers the army
1015 as intimately related to himself as a part of his own body,
in which he has been struck a wounding blow.

1016 *man of sorrows*: a not altogether satisfactory equivalent for
the compound Greek word, of which a closer translation
would be "greatly struck by Ruin" (*Atē*, which may also
have the connotation of "mad frenzy").

1020ff A thoroughly Aeschylean periphrasis for "quiver."

1025 This line gives strongest support to the view that Aeschylus
is in some sense covering up the Ionian Greeks' presence in

ANTISTROPHE 5

XERXES *Too warlike are they. I looked on a tragedy*
Unforeseen—

CHORUS *You speak of the rout of the throng of warships?*

XERXES *And rent my robes at the sight of the disaster.* 1030

CHORUS *Oh oh, oh oh!*

XERXES *And even more than Oh!*

CHORUS *For the ills are double and even threefold.*

XERXES *Grievous, but joys to our foes.*

CHORUS *And strength was shorn off—* 1035

XERXES *I am naked and stripped of escorts.*

CHORUS *By disasters at sea that our dear ones suffered.*

STROPHE 6

XERXES *Wet, wet your cheeks for the suffering, and go*
    to your homes. 1038

XERXES' army (see note on 950–61). By the date of this play, Themistocles' plan to dislodge them from the Persian empire had begun to take effect. Most of them had been "liberated" and were charter members of Athens' Delian League. (See further, my *Political Background*, pp. 17–21.)

1026 *Too warlike:* a fairly safe emendation for the strange form in the manuscripts.

1030 For tearing of the robe, see 468 and the QUEEN's vision, 199.

1034 That one's misfortunes were *joys to our foes* was a commonplace Greek expression from Homer down; likewise the converse, that one's own bliss caused "grief to enemies."

1035 The image is perhaps that of lopping off standing ears of grain or pruning trees.

111

CHORUS *I wet my cheeks in lamentation.* (1047)

XERXES *Raise a cry to echo mine.* 1040

CHORUS *A sorrowful response to sorrows.*

XERXES *Sound your shrieks along with me.*

CHORUS and XERXES *Oh oh, Oh oh, Oh oh, Oh oh!*

XERXES *Heavy is the misfortune.*

CHORUS *Ah! This too fills me with pain.* 1045

ANTISTROPHE 6

XERXES *Row, row your arms like oars and groan in
behalf of me.* 1046

CHORUS *Ah ah, pain, pain.* (1039)

XERXES *Raise a cry to echo mine.* 1048

CHORUS *Our concern attends you, master.*

XERXES *Raise up shrilly now your sobs.* 1050

CHORUS and XERXES *Oh oh, Oh oh, Oh oh, Oh oh!*

1039 This line stands as 1047 in the manuscripts, but it clearly
fits better here, after 1038 (the fact that lines 1040 and
1048 are identical may have caused the misplacement).

1041 Out of four words in the line, three mean "sorrowful."

1043 That the wail was uttered by XERXES and the CHORUS in
unison is suggested by the wording of 1042.

1044– I have accepted the manuscripts' indication of speakers,
1045 although some difficulties are thus created for the corresponding 1052–53, which would be better delivered by the
same speaker.

1046 *Row, row:* The metaphor is recurrent in Greek poetry. On
the physical manifestations of mourning, see note on 1062.

1051 I have assigned this line, on the model of 1043, to XERXES
and the CHORUS in unison.

XERXES   *Black will be the mixture—*

CHORUS   *Ah! Of groans and blows that fall.*

STROPHE 7

XERXES   *And strike your breast and cry aloud a Mysian
strain.*

CHORUS   *Oh sorrow, sorrow.*   1055

XERXES   *Tear the whitening hair of your beard.*

CHORUS   *Firm, firm is my grip, shrill my lament.*

XERXES   *Raise a sharp scream.*

CHORUS   *This too I shall do.*

ANTISTROPHE 7

XERXES   *And gash the robe at your breast with the points
of your hands.*   1060

CHORUS   *Oh sorrow, sorrow.*

1052– A closer translation would be "a black blow causing [or
1053   accompanied by] groans, will be mixed." Why "black"?
       The adjective may indicate that the blow is caused by
       "black" despair, and also results in "black" bruises. Perhaps
       both lines are spoken by the CHORUS: see note on 1044–
       45.

1054   Cf. note on 939. The Scholiast notes that "the Mysians and
       Phrygians were especially prone to lamentations," and there
       are other references in Greek literature to "Asiatic" styles
       of mourning.

1055   *sorrow, sorrow* here and at 1061 is the almost certain
       emendation that Gilbert Murray obtained by shifting an
       accent mark in the manuscript.

113

XERXES *And pluck at your hair and pity the troops.*

CHORUS *Firm, firm is my grip, shrill my lament.*

XERXES *Send floods from your eyes.*

CHORUS *I weep as you ask.*   1065

EPODE

XERXES *Raise a cry to echo mine.*

CHORUS *Oh oh! Oh oh!*

XERXES *Shout oh! and go to your homes.*

CHORUS *Oh oh!*

XERXES *Send a shout through the city.*   1070

CHORUS *Yes, yes, a shout indeed.*

XERXES *Lament with delicate step.*

CHORUS *Oh oh! The Persian land is painful to step upon.*

XERXES *Ah ah! Three-tiered were the ships*

1062 The CHORUS has been urged to indulge in the usual physical
      manifestations of mourning, not only wails but beating of
      the breast (1046, 1054), plucking the hair of their beards
      (1056), rending their garments (1060, to match XERXES'),
      and weeping (1064). Here they are told to "strum" their
      hair, "the plucking hands of the mourner being compared
      to those of a musician playing on a stringed instrument"
      (H. J. Rose).

1068 The CHORUS is dismissed.

1070 The city is Susa, as elsewhere in the play.

1072– *with delicate step:* introduces at the end a compound used
1074   frequently in the earlier parts of the play to suggest delicate
       luxury (cf. 42, 135 [with note on 133–39], 541, 543). The
       CHORUS replies that the Persian soil will hardly sustain them

Ah ah! By which they were destroyed.   1075

    CHORUS   *I shall escort you then with painful moans and cries.*

    The CHORUS and XERXES depart.

---

     in their grief. The two lines may indicate the refined dance measures that accompany the dirge.

1074– The play closes, fittingly, with a final reference to the
1075 *Three-tiered . . . ships* (see 679 and note on 664–71) that destroyed the Persian might at Salamis.

1076 The play ends with a solemn procession of the CHORUS from the orchestra (cf. the ending of *The Eumenides*).

APPENDIX

WAS THERE A *"SICILIAN TEXT"* OF THE PERSIANS?

In general, we are remarkably ill-informed about the circumstances of actual production of any ancient Greek tragedy. We are told, for example, by Plutarch (a late and not always reliable source) that Sophocles first entered the competitions in 468 B.C., that on this occasion the people honored the returning victorious general Cimon by allowing him and his fellow generals to judge the dramatic contest, and that Sophocles won over his more seasoned rival, Aeschylus; but we are not told the names of the winning plays. On the whole, what information we have is much less specific than this: a bare archondate in some late commentator's preface, or, in a few cases, the meagre details given by the fragmentary official victor lists on stone. About *The Persians* we know rather more: In addition to the inscriptional evidence for its performance at Athens in the spring of 472 B.C. with Pericles as producer (discussed in the "Introduction, pp. 8 and 19), we are told in one of the ancient "scholia" (marginal commentaries) on Aristophanes' *The Frogs*, line 1028, that *The Persians* was presented in Syracuse "at the urging of Hieron," ruler of that Sicilian city. As guarantor of this information, the Scholiast names the Alexandrian scholar Eratosthenes, who provided the detail in the third book of his work "On Comedies." The same information filtered down to the ancient anonymous *Life of Aeschylus* (paragraph 18), where the word "re-presented," "presented again," is substituted for the Scholiast's "presented." This may come closer to what Eratosthenes actually wrote and in any case fits in with the usual practice of

117

the Athenian tragic writers, to give a play its first "official" performance at the Great Festival of Dionysus at Athens and later repeat it
in one of the rural festivals of Attica or (as with *The Persians*) abroad.
So far, all seems clear. To an early trip to Hieron's court for the occasion of the dedication of the new city of Etna (probably in 475
B.C.), an event for which he composed a spectacle entitled *Women
of Etna*, Aeschylus added a second visit, and a second production of
The Persians, at some time after the Athenian production of 472.
(Aeschylus went to Sicily again, this time to Gela, towards the end
of his life, and died there; see C. J. Herington's article, "Aeschylus
in Sicily" in the *Journal of Hellenic Studies*, vol. 87, 1967.)

But the ancient Note on the passage in *The Frogs* creates more
problems than it helps to solve. Aristophanes makes Dionysus ex-
claim: "Yes, I really enjoyed it when I heard of the death *of Darius*,
and the Chorus clapped its hands together and said *Iauoi!*" (lines
1028–29). Apart from the metrical difficulties involved, *The Persians*
as we have it nowhere refers to the death of Darius, and nowhere in
it does the Chorus shout "iauoi," although the exclamation "iōa" occurs at 1070 and 1071. Scholars, beginnings with the Alexandrians, have
exercised a great deal of ingenuity in trying to explain the discrepancy.
Some early attempts can be traced in the same Scholion on the line,
mentioned above, and these will serve as a brief sketch of how ancient
literary scholars proceeded to "resolve" a problem of this kind. A
certain Chairis, a pupil of the great Aristarchus (the latter succeeded
to the headship of the Alexandrian library about 150 B.C.) attempted
—somewhat foolishly, as it appears—to explain that Aristophanes
meant "Xerxes" when he wrote "Darius," "for it was customary for
the poets to use the names of fathers instead of those of their sons."
It was sensibly pointed out (by whom the Scholiast does not say)
that this explanation will hardly do in view of the fact that it is explicitly stated at line 299 of our play that "Xerxes himself still lives
and looks upon the light." At some later date the scholar Herodicus
of Babylon, who wrote a work entitled "Individuals Satirized in
Comedy" and who seems to have taken generally a position opposite
to that of Aristarchus, attempted the following explanation: there were
two presentations, one containing a description of the battle of
Plataea (mentioned briefly at 816f. of our play). Since the quotation
from Herodicus is abridged and the Scholiast proceeds to mention
Eratosthenes' reference to the Sicilian production, we cannot tell
which version, the Athenian or the Sicilian, was on this hypothesis
the one which contained an allusion to the "death of Darius." In

any case, as the Scholiast continues, the theory was taken over by the scholar Didymus (called "Lead-belly" because of his prodigious industry), who worked at Alexandria in the first century B.C.; according to him, the version to which Aristophanes alludes "is not extant."

In fact, for all this learned theorizing, the lines in *The Frogs* give no support whatever to the hypothesis of a "Sicilian text," substantially different from that which we possess. Aristophanes has simply misremembered what actually occurs in *The Persians*, just as, a few lines earlier, he gets the order of Aeschylus' plays wrong. He mentions *The Seven Against Thebes* (producd in 467 B.C.) at 1021ff.; "*then, afterwards,* I presented *The Persians* . . . ," he has Aeschylus say (*The Frogs*, 1026). Aristophanes is writing a comedy, not a theatrical history, and didn't feel called upon to verify his facts down to the last detail. He and his audience remembered that *The Persians* was full of shouts and exclamations like "iauoi"; what matter to them that this word did not actually occur in the play?

The theory of a "Sicilian version" of the play is thus shown to rest on no evidence. With it must also be rejected any argument for a Sicilian slant in the remainder of the trilogy. On the basis of the information contained in the *Ancient Prefatory Note* (see p. 19) that the third play in the trilogy was entitled *Glaucus*, E. A. Freeman in his *History of Sicily* (1891) put forward the view that fragment 38 (Nauck), "chariot on chariot, corpses on corpses, horses on horses were all mixed in" (lines which are assigned to *Glaucus* by the Scholiast on Euripides' *The Phoenician Women*, 1194) comes from a description of the battle of Himera, where the Sicilians, under the command of Gelon, Hieron's brother and predecessor as ruler of Syracuse, repulsed a Carthaginian threat by land and sea; tradition had it that the victories of Himera and Salamis were won on the same day. Even without the removal of any support which a "Sicilian setting" for the trilogy might have given it, the theory should have fallen under the weight of the obvious fact that the fragment refers not to a hypothetical description of the historical battle of Himera, but of the mythical chariot race held at the funeral games for Pelias (Medea had persuaded his daughters to cut him up and boil him in a vain effort to rejuvenate him), in which Glaucus was torn to pieces by his own maddened mares (see "Introduction," p. 9); the scene is not Sicily, but near Iolkos in Thessaly. The weakness in Freeman's theory did not, however, prevent it from being taken over by modern scholars, who insist (wrongly, in my opinion) in trying to find a thematic connection between the plays in the trilogy. It has even been argued that

119

Phineus, the first play, "must have" contained some anticipation, perhaps in the form of an oracle, of the battles of 480 (the theory is put forward by Q. Cataudella, "Eschilo in Sicilia," *Dioniso* 26, 1963, pp. 19–22). Nor is there anything to be gained from pointing out that another of Aeschylus' *Glaucus*-plays seems to have mentioned various places in Sicily and Italy, including Himera (fragment 32, Nauck), for these references almost certainly come from *The Marine Glaucus*, probably a satyr-play, produced when and where we do not know but having no connection whatever with *The Persians*.

It is very easy to spin hypotheses of this kind. One might argue, for example, that because several fragmentary lines in *Glaucus of Potniae* contain references to the sea (specifically, Oxyrhynchus Papyrus XVIII. 2160, fr. 7 lines 2 and 8, fr. 9 line 6), Aeschylus somehow contrived an allusion to the battle of Artemisium, which had served as a prelude to Salamis. The games for Pelias, in which Glaucus unsuccessfully competed, were held near Iolkos, on the Gulf of Pagasae; it was on this gulf that the Persian fleet had sought an anchorage before setting out to confront the Greeks at the nearby headland of Artemisium. In addition, the Persian fleet anchored precisely at a spot connected with the legendary voyage of the Argonauts (Herodotus 7. 193), which was given some prominence—exactly how much we cannot tell—in *Phineus* (see "Introduction," p. 9). But the temptation to weave such fantasies must be resisted; they rest on no stronger support than does the theory of a "Sicilian setting."

BIBLIOGRAPHY

The detailed commentary by H. D. Broadhead (Cambridge, at the University Press, 1960) is indispensable, and seems likely to remain so for some time to come. On specific passages readers may wish to consult A. S. F. Gow, "Notes on the *Persae* of Aeschylus" in *Journal of Hellenic Studies* 48 (1928) 133–59. Useful discussions of the ghost-raising scene can be found in S. Eitrem, "The Necromancy in the Persai of Aeschylus," *Symbolae Osloenses* 6 (1928) 1–16, and H. J. Rose, "Ghost Ritual in Aeschylus," *Harvard Theological Review* 43 (1950) 257–80.

Recent articles on literary aspects of the play include Harry C. Avery, "Dramatic Devices in Aeschylus' *Persians*," *American Journal of Philology* 85 (1964) 173–84 (although it seems to me unlikely that, as Avery maintains, "1038 marks the point at which Xerxes put on new and undamaged robes" [182]); B. Alexanderson, "Darius in the *Persians*," *Eranos* 65 (1967) 1–11; and William C. Scott, "The Mesode at *Persae* 93–100," *Greek, Roman & Byzantine Studies* 9 (1968) 259–66.

G. Salanitro revives the theory that in the play Aeschylus is supporting Aristeides and the Conservatives, with their "politica filolaconica ed antipersiana," against Themistocles, who stood for "una politica egemonica, caratterizzata da un rilassamento della tensione nelle relazioni con i Persiani [!] a da un parallelo inasprimento dei rapporti con gli Spartani," "Il Pensiero Politico di

121

BIBLIOGRAPHY

Eschilo nei *Persiani*," *Giornale Italiano di Filologia* [Naples] 18 (1965) 193–235 (the citations are taken from page 233); for a refutation of this view I must again refer readers to my study, *The Political Background of Aeschylean Tragedy* (Ann Arbor, University of Michigan Press, 1966) Chapter II.

In a short, sensitive article, "Réflexions sur la tragédie des *Perses*," (*Information littéraire* 8 [1956] 15–18), Jacqueline Duchemin comments on the "sonorities of the exotic names" in the three catalogs at lines 16ff., 302ff. and 955ff. The last she compares to "the inscription on a cenotaph in its rapid conciseness." She well remarks that "instead of merely heightening for the Athenians the joy of their triumph and the realization of their deliverance, the poet invites them on the contrary to feel for the conquered enemy the sympathy of one human being for another in the face of the precariousness of their common existence" (17).

A doctoral thesis by H. D. Edinger, *Vocabulary and Imagery in Aeschylus' Persians* (Princeton, 1961), unfortunately did not come to my attention in time for me to use it in preparing my own commentary.